Between Fields and Stars

Also by Edmund Cusick

Gronw's Stone: Voices from the Mabinogion (with Ann Gray)
Blodeuwedd: An Anthology of Women's Poetry (editor)
Ice Maidens

Between Fields and Stars

Edmund Cusick

New & Selected
Poetry and Prose

edited by Gladys Mary Coles

HEADLAND

in association with
the Centre for Writing
Liverpool John Moores University

First published in 2008
by
HEADLAND PUBLICATIONS
38 York Avenue, West Kirby,
Wirral, Merseyside CH48 3JF

A full CIP record for this book is available
from the British Library

ISBN 1 902096 50 6

Printed in Great Britain by
L. Cocker Ltd,
Unit A9, Prospect St,
Liverpool L6 1AU

CONTENTS

Edmund Cusick was born in 1962 in Aberdeen, grew up in Bieldside and took a First Class in English at Aberdeen University. Oxford followed, where he read for his PhD and worked as a lexicographer for the Oxford English Dictionary. He fulfilled a dream when he moved to Wales (his mother's country), appointed as a Lecturer in English Literature at Lampeter, University of Wales. Here he took further his passionate interest in Celtic literature and spirituality, myth and legend, and began to develop his own talent as a storyteller.

In 1991 he moved to Liverpool, lecturing at the Polytechnic which became, shortly afterwards, Liverpool John Moores University. At LJMU, first as Course Leader, and later as Head of Department, he taught Imaginative Writing and built up the degree programme in this subject.

He published three books with Headland: *Gronw's Stone:Voices from the Mabinogion* with Ann Gray (1997); *Blodeuwedd: An Anthology of Women's Poetry* (2001); and *Ice Maidens* (2006). Winner of the Keats-Shelley Prize 2005 and the Housman Prize 1998, he was a runner-up in the Bridport Prize and other competitions. Edmund Cusick was also a co-editor and contributor to *The Writer's Workbook* (Arnold 2000; second edition 2004). He married Christina Crabtree and they lived with their daughters at Hendrw Bridge, Llandrillo, in Denbighshire. He died on 15 January 2007, at the age of forty-four.

INTRODUCTION

The title *Between Fields and Stars* is drawn from 'January', the last poem in *Ice Maidens*, Edmund Cusick's first full collection, published shortly before his death. When I was sadly planning his Memorial Service, and feeling, with many others, 'the dismay of broken music', the idea came that I could put together a new volume of his work. As his publisher, friend and colleague at the university, I knew of his writing in publications other than his three Headland books; and I felt sure that there was unpublished work among his files and papers. The idea for the new book and its title occurred in one epiphanic moment.

I am immensely grateful to Christina Cusick for making her husband's papers available and giving me access to his journal. As a result, new poems and prose appear in *Between Fields and Stars* and are complementary to the previously published work. Giving coherence to the whole is the distinctive voice and vision of Edmund Cusick. The new poems, with their agile language and sensuous imagery, stand in significant relation to those in *Ice Maidens*. 'Sea of Ice', a major sequence, was intended for inclusion in *Ice Maidens* but was not finished in time for publication. 'Lament', written for his small daughters, is a deeply moving valedictory poem.

When preparing the section of new poems, I was grateful to Ann Gray, co-author with Edmund of *Gronw's Stone: Voices from the Mabinogion,* for her careful sifting and organising of some unpublished poems which were in variant versions, work which she regarded as 'a huge privilege'. Ann Gray has also contributed an Introduction to my selection from *Gronw's Stone*, in which four of the poems written by Edmund accompany the stories of the Four Branches. He considered his writing on myth, and especially his extended study of Blodeuwedd and her manifestations, to be of central importance in his work.

Mark Wynn, a close friend whom Edmund met at Oxford, and with whom he had many shared interests, has contributed 'A Memoir' which, with its keen insight into Edmund's mind and character, provides an illuminating prelude.

While, in his academic career Edmund Cusick achieved much in a relatively short time, he was also building a national reputation as a poet. His award-winning 'Speaking in Tongues' (the Keats-Shelley Prize 2005) and 'Ny Alesund' (the Housman Prize 1998) are included here in my selection from *Ice Maidens*, described by John Burnside as 'a marvellous collection'. The selected poems exemplify essential elements in his work: recurring themes, a confluence of the erotic and the spiritual, skilful deployment of voice and persona, an acute ear for dialogue and when to use it. A notable success during his final year was the enthusiastic reception of his paper 'Art, Imagination and Psyche: A Journey by Water' at the University of Greenwich's Jung Conference. This paper, a Jungian interpretation of poems in *Ice Maidens*, will be published by Routledge in *Psyche and the Arts*, edited by Dr Susan Rowlands.

John Burnside's fine poem in memory of Edmund, 'Shape shifters' first published in *Agenda* in 2007, closes the present volume.

Between Fields and Stars should prove of enduring value and inspiration not only to those who already know and enjoy Edmund Cusick's work, but also to the new readers whom I hope it will attract.

Gladys Mary Coles

A Memoir

Edmund was a dreamer. And like most dreamers he was sometimes inclined to impracticality - involving shoelaces, or a grown man tumbling through a ceiling...

But Edmund was of course no ordinary dreamer…

In Oxford he was making a professional study of dreams, examining the works of George MacDonald in the light of Carl Jung's theories of the unconscious. And at that time he would record his own dreams daily and examine them in Jungian terms.

For most of us dreams have to do with unreality, but for Edmund it was our unexamined everyday waking world that was shadowy and insubstantial, and dreams that pointed towards the true nature of things.

There is a famous parable set down in Plato's Republic of a man who leaves behind his fellows who are confined to a cave and spend their days watching shadows play upon the walls of the cave, while supposing that this is the sum of reality – and the man leaves the cave and reaches the world of sunlight, and eventually he is able to train his gaze upon the sun. And having seen the true nature of things he resolves to return to the cave, in part to share his enlightenment with his former companions, but they laugh at him as his eyes struggle to adjust once more to the darkness, and seeing his practical disorientation they think of him as someone who has no true conception of what the world is about and what demands it makes upon us.

I like to think of Edmund's impracticality in these terms (as the disorientation of someone whose eyes are accustomed to a brighter light). Of course he had a keen interest in celestial and astrological phenomena, and while he may not have gazed directly at the sun, his life stands as a record of one man's persevering and, in my experience anyway, unparalleled attempt to see beyond the surface appearance of things, beyond the shadows, so as to grasp what really matters in a human life.

Plato thought of course that the person who had seen the sun (and here he had in mind above all Socrates), was in a way the most practical of all. And I think this is true of Edmund.

At Oxford he had many dreams for his own future – he dreamt that he would find a woman with whom he could share his life and who would love him as deeply as he loved her. He dreamt that they would have a family of girls (he could have made do with boys of course but certainly he dreamt of girls). He dreamt that he would live in rural Wales within earshot of a mountain brook, and he dreamt that he would take on the mantle of his uncle Gwill, his mother's brother (who had also lived in Wales) and become a poet. And he dreamt that somehow the established conventions of university life would give way and that he would be able to teach a course that was as much about spiritual formation and self-discovery as it was about a command of facts and modes of inference. And of course all of this, although undeniably the stuff of dreams (of rampant fantasy really), all of this came to pass – and this leads me to think that Edmund although a dreamer, or perhaps because a dreamer, was more attuned to what this world might have to offer, was more attuned to its practical potentialities, than are the rest of us – when we cast aside our dreams and make compromises of many kinds in the name of achieving a reconciliation with what we call 'reality'.

Edmund had a keen sense of place, and his life is a story of his love for and identification with particular places. And his friendships were very often embedded in a shared sensibility for particular places – this was true of course of the trips he made with his writing students – in introducing them to the places he loved (such as Clynnog) he was introducing you to himself. Among places his earliest love was of course Bieldside in Aberdeen – and his enduring and passionate attachment to that place was inseparable from his enduring and passionate attachment to his mother and father, and to his sisters Rhiannon and Eleri. And there was also his attachment to Oxford, to Port Meadow, and New College Cloister and elsewhere, and to the hills around Aberdeen, and to many other places. In all of these respects Edmund showed himself to be no mere dreamer but someone who could (once again) take hold of our everyday waking world and conjure from it a reality that was made in his own image – and it was for this reason that his gift of himself in friendship was often indistinguishable from his gift to his friends of certain places, together with his own sensitivity for those places.

Among Edmund's dreams was the possibility of an afterlife, of a spiritual world always connected to our bodily experience, but not reducible to it. And if one wanted some kind of 'proof' of such an afterlife, which Edmund himself did not, one could do no better than to look to his life – in all of the ways I have been describing, Edmund's dreams have offered (for me anyway) a deeper intimation of the nature of things than the apparently real but really insubstantial set of 'facts' that very often counts as reality. So perhaps in this matter too Edmund the dreamer will prove to be more alive to our possibilities than are so called 'realists'.

In any case we know from his poems that Edmund had come to love Hendwr and the Berwyns and the people of this place, and that, as was his custom, he soaked himself into this particular landscape. And we know therefore that whenever we step into this landscape, and enjoy it in the spirit of Edmund's poems, and see it as dreamily vouchsafing some account of human possibilities, we know that in all of this we will encounter Edmund – our friend and guide, our Socrates, dreamer, visionary, and man of sound practical sense.

Mark Wynn

New Poems

The Old Stars

for Storm (Imogen)

I want to teach her the old stars,
to be the one to trace these patterns

in the cold hours of the dark,
her small hand at my sleeve,

to show her the perpetual surprise
of stars above these fields and hills,

the one to say, *see, there's his belt,*
and at my voice stars dance

into beasts, the Eagle, the Lion,
Cygnus, the great bird, the swan;

Herne the Hunter, rising in the east,
his glittering antlers, blue and white

his loins a smear of light and, glinting
at his feet, the hound of death,

the brightest promise in the sky;
the shape the people call the wain

the plough, the seven stars
the knuckled hand of God;

and in the West, the salmon
twisting its starry tail, the seven

water sprites swimming in the mist
too swift to count. They'll wrap around us,

legions of them, forgotten stars from
before the cities, before childhood,

crowding over the trees, sheltering in
that familiar dome, the long river of the milky way.

A Prayer for a Christening

for Amber

Listen. The world is being born afresh
in the eyes and ears of Amber.
Each day it is being made
a little more. Earth parts from water,
air from rain, moon and sun reveal themselves.

Into this world come beech leaves and bluebells,
the wren who hides by the river,
dragonflies over the pool.
Today you are in it.

Out of this world we draw our prayer.
May the holy spirit bless you
with the wisdom of the snake, the gentleness of the dove,
the strength of earth, the power of fire,
the beauty of ice, the grace of the wind,
the music of water, the cleverness of fox,
the knowledge of wolf, the playfulness of jackal,
the purity of silver, the warmth of amber.

May angels keep you.
May moon and stars light your way.
May darkness and dawn be friends to you.
May heaven and earth embrace you
and grant you joy.

Special Edition

for Abi

You sat beside your mother
as she drove. From the back
seat, the driving mirror showed
only your eyes, at once grown wise,
smiling, bemused, as though
surprised by love's response.
Till, when you spoke, I recognised
my error. Yet my mistake
was true, for in that moment
I saw the mother who would be
my wife, loved her in you.

Erotolepsy

Thomas Hardy coined
this word. Used it
once, supplied
an explanatory note:
a violent seizure
of desire.
When I watch you
pull on your tight red
gloves, I put it back
into the language.

The Red Suede Skirt

made you smile, blush,
as you unwrapped it
from swathes of tissue
paper. You said,
You make me feel
like a kept woman.
Fine, I thought, if
that means I keep you.

Haute parfumerie

Paris, L'Aeroport Charles de Gaulle.
Caught between flights, languages,
thirsty for English,
I am seduced in the duty free
by whispered French
Oh La La! Je t'adore!
Champagne! Paris! Volupté!
Mystère. Je Reviens -
and a tongue that's half
familiar: *Globe. Polo. Red.*
Not *English* English, but the esperanto
of transatlantic dreams, flashing up
the flights of fancy,
alternative departures;
Figi Dakaar Byzance Egypt Kashmir.
Each signed in calligraphic
hand, each a *Poème:*
Obsession.
Potent words, administered
in single drops, or vaporised
into a mist of meaning:
Sun Moon and Stars. Incense. Parfum Sacré.
Elements
alchemy to work our base desires
into the scents of faith. It is not sex
that sells, but innocence. Shorn
of our gods, we long for paradise:
Arden, Elysium, Shangri-La,
Cool Water, Fleur d'Interdite, Eternity,
Eden.
Manchester. My flight is called.
Burdened with bags, I turn
for one last look,
Obsession. Wings. Escape.

Harvest

The borders. Through the windscreen
the hill's stark outline and the moon.
You drove, hunched tense to the wheel
guessing the deceitful twists of road
the unseen verges of friendship,
something else. The way
obscured by shadows.

Put the headlights out, I said, not meaning it.

You did. Moonlight flooded the road,
that swollen moon embracing the Wrekin,
hesitant on our pale hands. I wound
the window down, and we smelled Shropshire
rich with hay, dried dung, the night hedgerows
awash with honeysuckle, meadowsweet,
coils of corn piled high. Ahead, another road
lit by the moon, a leaning gate, two lines
curving together, winding to the trees.

The mirror blind with light, a horn, a snarl of brakes.
You swerved and swore, snapped the lights on,
pulled out, swore again. He passed us, shouting
and after him, car after car, till you took me home,
unspeaking, did not return my call.

Yet that night, as I slept, we left the lane,
drove through stookes and sheaves,
passed through the open gate
to that first forest and under circled oaks,
stopped, felt the light moth-flutter of our tongues.

St David's

None of us expected it, not from the maps.
A hollow of the past, and something older,
the trembling of moist air, a river
slipping over stones set by monks
as though the water was still theirs.

Above, the trees soft with lichen and decay,
jackdaws guarding broken twigs, cold,
peace. Their complaining a part of this silence
spun from time and prayer, and from
forgetting. A well in time, drawing
deeper than memory, into the lingering
souls of those who imagined it, prayed for it,
found it at last, at the edge of the world: pilgrims.

The sick, seeking a spring
older than Christ, came here, finding
fresh water within sight of the sea, heavy
with mineral on the tongue, brimming over
the copper that wished it into holiness,
the green metal making a chain of hopes
in the magical coinage of prayer.

My coin does not sink straight,
but darts a moment, as if alive, in a clear current.
Pilgrims still come, seeking healing, rest,
God, even finding him, perhaps, in a place
inhabited by birds, in the flame burning
over a saint's bones, in sunlight
stealing over high walls, making the stone live.

May

all is fire
fire in the air
fire in all things flesh
liquid fire coiled
in the heart of water
black water burning
purple saxifrage
violet light
grass moss and lichen
water lightning

Delphinus

I watch as smooth grey backs
split the cold waters of the firth.
A fisherman observes
All other creatures shun man
but they come to us.
Their greeting troubles,
as though evidence of some long broken
covenant of sea and man.

Once the bond was real. In the palace of Knossos
your snub-nosed smile is inlaid
tile by jewelled tile. Christians
etched you on communion cups, symbol of devotion.
Zeus took dolphin shape to swim upstream
and found the shrine of Delphi;
in the blue Aegean you befriended triremes.
Their master mariners mapped our stars,
and found their pilot there: Delphinus
leaping with twisting tail to the pale
milky way, which charts
the soul's last voyage.

Those stars eclipse now,
our skies, our seas, polluted,
our planet pilotless.

Jackal

Take this jackal headed
friend as token of the one
who swiftly runs unspoken
paths which snake through
labyrinths of space
and time. If you miss me
let him scent me out.
And when you wake; or half
awake, or dream; or think
you hear his dog-thought echoing
your own, or sense the prick
of ears whose points rise sharp
beneath a pyramided dark,
and hear him listening,
silent, sphinx like,
to hear your breathing slow
and deep, and when the brush
of short fur stirs on your skin,
you spill the night's cold share
into her water dish, take care
of the attentive one who drinks
as well, from what you fill;
his gentle tongue licks
the hands of those
who wait for us beyond,
and finds them sweeter far
than water under desert stars,
shining clear and still.
Listen my love, and pour
from your heart's overflow
a bowl for he who guards
our life, and those quick eager
lives growing between our own.

Children of Dark

Those children born
at midwinter, wail
at the sun's first rising.
Their eyes, paler than ice
bluer than amethyst,
know a world of snow, stars.
They draw themselves to
the breast of the dark
and as night comes,
welcome it.

North

North is our creed, our belief,
North is the divine point,
the end of journeying,
the cardinal direction
to which the sun burns,
the earth disappears,
the deepest darkness rests.

Dressing for the Arctic

Thin socks, cotton; thick socks, wool;
underwear, thermal, long; vest, thermal,
ribbed; shirt, long-sleeved, wool;
jersey, double-knit, wool;
trousers, over-trousers, waterproof;
parka, padded, with Gore-Tex outer shell
and drawstring hood; gloves, inner,
cotton; gloves, insulated, waterproof;
boots; sunscreen, factor thirty; sunglasses,
UV protective; snowgoggles, scarf.

Only the teeth are naked.

When she smiles, my teeth hurt.

Sea of Ice

Prologue

In 1594, Willem Barents, sailing in search of the North East passage to China, became the first Western navigator to cross the Arctic seas to Novaya Zemlya. Inexplicably, on the west coast of the island, Barents found the remains of a European settlement. Later, contact with the native Samoyed people revealed the story of a party of Europeans who had landed there from a single ship years before, and were said to have provoked an attack in which many were killed.

The identity and fate of this ship remain unknown. One theory is that it belonged to Jacob Cornelisz, the leader of a Dutch religious sect who had prophesied that the world would not be redeemed until the gospel had been preached to the last remnants of the survivors of the flood. These, he believed, still inhabited the unexplored Polar regions. Having chartered a ship from Amsterdam in 1568, Cornelisz and six of his followers disappeared from record.

I

First came the dream.
Another desert, flayed
by a freezing sun,
and, bobbing in a violet sea,
unclean beasts, their dog heads
those the prophet saw,
howling forever, outside
the walls of the eternal city -
then one, the son of man,
brighter, whiter than snow,
heard his voice saying,
leave all and follow me.

who held in his hands the seven stars
find those who live in darkness
untouched by the blood of the lamb

and in our crofts, our farms,
we woke, knew we had each
shared the dream, heard
the larks above our fields,
our cattle complaining,
smelled Columbine, cornflower,
knew that the Lord had spoken,
that we must find this last parish,
this unholy land
at the edges of his world,
a race of men dwelling on ice.

Tonight we return to bid farewell
to cattle, farms, arrange our business.
We have been chosen.

II

In Amsterdam we seek the wisdom
of the cosmographers.
In the universities of Vilnius, Riga
scholars define the world with charts
scored and pocked with lines,
with numbers, yet where
we point, their globes are empty,
crowned with foolish drawings,
imagined mountains rising
from conjectured deeps;
monsters spouting, *mare incognito.*
They posit here a final point, *axis mundi,*
at which the round world makes
a cross of many rays, the pole
to which our needles spin,
which stirs the sleeping will in iron
and to whose voice the mote
of lodestone in the goose skull answers,
its every flight a straying or return.

It is the last realm,
remote even beyond greed.
No whaler, no man of war has ever
returned from the shifting chaos of the ice:

those latitudes are impenetrable
uninhabitable, a waste.

There, creation runs without
purpose. There, absolute love
beats uselessly in barren seas,
laps against empty shores.

The northern sea is impassable

as was, we do not doubt, Genneseret
in the tempest, The Red Sea also.
So God's forgiveness ends
with their knowledge, at
the seventieth degree of latitude.

But we have our own charts,
given in the tongues of angels,
drawn in visions. We know
their fabled pole the furthest
point from Calvary, true centre
of this world, from which
all trespassing is measured.

It is a place of death where
nothing lives, the region of the bear.
There the sea yields to ice, the air
to hail. Mountains of fire pierce
sea and sky. It is a desert
where rivers flow through barren
wastes, of earth bleached white
by perpetual light, or darkness.

In its shadow live those we must redeem
before the world can rest.
And hearing our word, the faithful give
salt pork, silver, rope, dogs,
tallow, timber, nails.

III

We have a ship. The master weighs
our calling, as he would ballast,
and finds us wanting. He fears no God.
For crew he picks profane men
whose finest longing is for the rum
and whores of Amsterdam.
At the furthest stretch of storm, or ice,
they are less like to mutiny, *mewling*
for bastards or womenfolk behind.

IV

The circle of darkness, the region
of the bear. At the seventy first degree,
leviathan broke our wake,
its tail curved smooth for thirteen fathoms,
vanished in the deeps.

At seventy four degrees
ice masses in the water
grinds against the hull, disperses.
In the hold, dogs whine and vomit.

At seventy six degrees the ice
becomes blue, green moulded
and misshapen, half created.
At night salt frosts burn our flesh,
but the days lengthen, six minutes, eight.

At seventy seven degrees,
Ursa Major stands above our heads,
endless and circling.
Here direction begins
and ends in water. The ice
drifts uncharted in continents,
shifting continually.
But the Lord guides us
each day showing us a way,
and each next day
the grey drifts close behind us.

The doves we brought to spy out land
will not leave. Today we found them
twisted, stiff-winged on the deck.
The ravens curse us in their cages,
beg for scraps of meat.

Landfall. From the mist, rise cliffs,
screaming with a legion of birds,
rocks bare of all green, save the bright
slime that grows from their excrement.

V

The shore is barren. Sheer cliffs dwarf
our huts. Our promised land, a wilderness
of ice, shale and scurvy grass.

We read the prophets, meditate
on lands of olives, wells
among the dust. *I will give you*
the water of life. There is no pillar
of fire by night, or smoke by day,
no spring bursting the dry rock
to spatter on the sand,
no manna to fall as snow
on faithful hands. We do not
hear him in the grind of floe
on floe nor see him in the bare cliffs
rising from the sea, the sun
a torture of perpetual light,
the stars a soft curve in the dark.

We dream of trees, of cats
basking in the sun, of gardens,
buttercups between the cobbles
on Schuestraase, the grocer's
daughter playing with her hoop,
red flowers in the wheat.

Our privies have bequeathed
a rash of grass upon the tundra.
The ravens thrive, nesting
in the cliffs. They love us
less now, having learnt to quarrel
with the foxes for the carcass
of the reindeer.

VI

The sun sets neither on our anger
nor our faith. The liturgy of time
that sifts the Sabbath
from the common day is lost.
In Amsterdam they calculate the hour
of right ascension and declension
of pagan stars, plotting exact degrees
of fantasy; the sun would set
in the sign of the Fishes,
or at the rising of Procyon
on the twenty sixth of April.

We grow cunning in calculations
of our own, measuring the growth
of beard, of fingernails.
Some have begun to count months
also, fearing this day will never end.

We take the boats, search for huts,
villages, find nothing.

VII

Here time has its hollows,
its secret chambers. As light
burns through the glaciers we see
the quartz-white skulls of seals,
walrus, perfect, uncorrupted,
lodged in turquoise crystal.
We see also those of creatures
we do not recognise, older
than the flood. In one we find
an arrow head, and on a beach,
a rough cairn raising a bear's head,
half decayed, its empty sockets
gazing North.

VIII

On the day the sun set
we saw against its fire, the temple
of their abominations, crowning
a promontory like briar's spikes.
We landed, found it a thicket
of rude sticks thrust
in the mud, cuts gouged
for mouth and eyes. In the centre
the upended, hollow neck bone
of a whale, open, obscene, facing
North to the quarter of darkness.

The pastor threw it down, rooted up the idols
broke them, made a cross.
He carries this before us. From this Golgotha
a mess of tracks: hooves, feet. We follow.

IX

On the third day, we saw on the horizon
lines of men moving to the shore
and in the evening, came upon them.
There in the whirling storm of gulls
a beached whale, its belly slashed
to purple flaps of meat, stinking
of the sea. And heaving from the ruined
ribs, their children, faces rimmed
with gore, dragging out its offal,
and the heathen, slant eyed, shouting
in the tongue of Babel, quick
and high pitched, as though in chant.

The souls we had been promised.

I had dreamed of this. At such hours I know
Angels have come to aid God's chosen.
I prayed then for some sudden sign
or the swift gift of tongues. Instead,
a rush of arrows, barbs, tearing at clothes and flesh,
sailors running for the rocks, loading muskets
while we stood sure in faith, crying for calm, the hiss
and click of powder, damp, misfiring, the confusion
of tongues and prayer, our calling on the Lord,
the pastor turning in the mud,
shots tearing the air apart.

After, only one of them remained
alive, twisting at some sorcerous thing
about his neck, repeating the same sounds over
and over, till the sailors cut them short.

X

Of the chosen, only I survive, saved
for this punishment; to see my brethren slaughtered.

I struggle with the mystery of martyrdom:
the Lord who fashioned us in love,
even in the womb, calls us to him
to be destroyed.

We were not promised glory, only
a task we must fulfil.

Do this to save the world, to save yourselves.

Their blood cries out against this place
for testimony. Marked by some special grace
or sin, I live, unworthy, shameful.

My task to say the good words over the graves
while the boat crew stand guard, my task to
hand them silver coins, in return for their denial,
should any ask them, of these deaths, my life.

XI

South, but the nights grow longer
the ice thicker, as though
it spawned around us. Frost
wounds our hands and feet;
men climb the masts, palms
bandaged in strips of cloth.
We run against winter now,
taste it in the freezing mist
scourging our lungs.
We sail with double watch
and open gunports,
cannon slathering with spume,
dogs' snouts to nose the scents
of those we came to save.

XII

The master's mourning was short,
as he has other duties. His charts
mark our course for his return.
In his cabin the world grows
under his pen, finds shape and name.
Here, he writes, the Cape of Geese, here,
the Bay of Silence. Hidden in his voice
I hear the lust for warm currents,
lands of silk and spices.

Let there be idols enough among them,
if only they be cast from gold.

So too, I coveted converts
to mouth the name of Christ.

Lazarus

Listen. After the pain, blackness
rushing, and in the whirling
dark, a star, drawing me
within, opening
into the heart of light,
white, radiant, as pearl.

This is the pearl he spoke of
the one the merchant found, precious
above all else.
I have seen it.

And beyond, my father
greeting me, a city raised
in Amethyst and Sapphire.
Angels clothed in golden light.
I wept.

Then the Rabbi's voice, calling my name,
drawing me through the dark
to the stench of that close tomb,
my hands tearing at the cloth
that bound my eyes.
Tears on all their faces
and on his own.

Now, as each sun dies
I wait, to hear him call
my name again, impatient,
longing
for that bright land.

Lament

All I can leave you are words
and words are not enough.

I have made a life out of words,
I know words are not enough.

You don't need words, you need
a father beside you, a father

watching over you, a father
to be suspicious of your first boyfriends,

a father who can shake the hand
of the first one he trusts, a father

to teach you the names of the stars,
how to fix them when the country is strange

and you need a direction, a father
to teach you how to make a fire,

how to douse it with sand or wet grass,
a father to hear what you discover of the world,

a father to answer your questions with answers
that will not always make sense, till maybe later.

I have been hopelessly ill equipped
to find my way around this world, though

I knew the words for almost everything.
I have not led a life that is ordinary.

I was born for an understanding of the worlds
beyond this flimsy one of wire and streetlight,

the darker and brighter worlds.
I've spoken in tongues and I may do still.

I have met the spirits of Fire and Water.
Anubis has visited my dreams. I've known

the sacred places. I am not alone.
Spirits sit by me now, as I write.

They'll let you find your own way, my children,
but they will always be near you.

On Poetry

Part of the reward of poetry comes in the peculiar intimacy with which we sense the poet's presence. In poetry we step into another consciousness in a peculiarly intense way. English poetry is not so much the art of imaginative creation as of perception. While fiction may offer escape from our existence, poetry pulls in precisely the opposite direction, requiring of us that we review the stuff of human life with a new intensity.

In a post-Christian culture, in which the sense of a higher order has faded or disappeared, this concern with intense apprehension affords poetry a unique seriousness. …Such events as the death of Princess Diana precipitated a wave of tributes in verse from people who might never before have written poetry, and indeed poetry is one of the few mediums in which mourning is allowed public expression. Poetry of course is as various as the artists who create it, but collectively, it is fair to say that poetry has come to hold a place as a kind of secular meditation, a shifting of focus – a catching of the breath before some image or event which by its nature throws light on all around it. To describe this function critics employ a word drawn from the lexicon of religious experience: epiphany….

Poetry at its most intense is a torchlit journey, the poet's oblique and twisting paths from thought to thought, word to word, precipitating synaptic leaps in the reader's brain. Thus poetry commonly requires a greater degree of concentration from the reader than does prose, and thus deliberate disturbances in common logic, such as paradox and synaesthesia, are native to poetry….

Metaphor

Metaphor is a kind of magic worked in the alembic of the imagination – conjuring and mating the natures of disparate things: apricots cool as plants of gilded snow, a girl's body as sweet cherry blossom, jonquil light. Equally, magic can be read as no more than the literal enactment of things conjured by metaphor. *He howled like a wolf*, the poet might write; but the voice of children's story and fireside tale would whisper, he *was* a wolf.

from the Introduction to Firesigns *by Rose Flint (Poetry Salzburg, 2004)*

On Poetry and Alchemy

Alchemy breaks down conventional perceptions of the world and replaces them with a radically different understanding based on personal revelation. This reconfiguration of perception can be compared to the creative process. One theory of poetry asserts that poetry is therapeutic, and pleasurable, because it makes connections between the left and right brain. Language belongs to the left brain, emotion to the right; our sense of logic and order to the left, our sense of rhythm, of pattern, and of colour, to the right. Poetry, it is argued, enables connections between these modes of thought. To give the simplest possible example, we can see this process at work in a single literary device: the transferred epithet.

We can make poetry simply by taking a word from one place, the logical or correct place, and putting it in another, in a way that 'scrambles' the logic of the piece but makes it into poetry. For example, in *Birthday Letters*, Ted Hughes writes of standing at a cliff edge in the wind feeling 'the blue push of the sea'. The push is the pressure of the wind; and is not blue. It has no colour at all, but the view seen by the poet, while pushed, has. The deliberate confusion of the two senses results, like an impressionist painting, in a more complete vision of what the poet experienced. Another example of this reordering of thought through interference with the logical order of language comes, as it did in alchemy, in paradox.

Again, Ted Hughes, describing the fox cub's image of the night, writes of 'the huge whisper of the constellations'. A whisper is by definition small, slight. For a whisper to be huge defies logic but inspires an illogical wonder at the faint yet awesome patterns of the overarching night sky. These devices offer us a microcosm of what poetry does. What is in our heads is not the logic of language; it is the chaos of feeling. But to express it we need the logic of language. Poetry supplies something closer to what is within our heads than prose, or logic, can. Poetry and alchemy could thus both be said to work towards changes in consciousness. The best image of this process is probably Coleridge's great metaphor of the imagination in the opening lines of Chapter Fourteen of *Biographia Literaria*: that of the effect of sunlight or moonlight on a landscape which we thought was familiar. The scene is physically the same but our perception of it acquires new significance, new patterns, new harmonies, and indeed, beauty.

Alchemy offers us an instance, a paradigm, of how the apparent world can be broken down and reinterpreted, as the eye of poetic vision does. The practice of alchemy is in a sense a distillation of a principle of the artist's calling: to see through apparent reality into the truth beneath. Both poetry and alchemy insist on a thing having an apparent nature, and a deeper nature, that reveals itself to an eye that has itself undergone an inner transformation. Poetry naturally seeks a meaningfulness in things: Hughes' cub is literally a foxcub but it is also a sign, a portent of his marriage... Poetry offers a reading of the world we inhabit - not just observing it, but interpreting its meaning.

On Myth

Myths are the first stories, the mother and father of all the stories that follow. The age of myths is measured not in years but in thousands of years. Within myths are experiences and intuitions so powerful that they grow while being told and retold down the generations. Myths are stories which encode intuitions of the way the world is. Every culture has myths to explain our first beginnings: the Yoruba myth of the first men coming to earth on a ladder spun by a spider, or the Indian story of Yama and Yami, the first man and woman, or the Hebrew story of the Garden of Eden.

Why use myths? Why breath oxygen? We have no choice. To tell stories is as natural to us as breathing. We are, in a sense, made of stories: every culture in every age has told them, and our stories form our understanding of ourselves and of the world. We may have swapped the campfire for the soap opera, tales of marvels for gossip and urban legends, but our hunger for stories remains as keen as ever. Even soap opera plots develop mythic dimensions: the body under the patio, the secret act of incest, can, for a week or a month, grip the collective imagination...

Myth is more than a body of stories, it is a way of associating with an inner, intuitive order rather than the cold logic of fact. It is peculiarly responsive to both the creative imagination and the unconscious.

Myth, though often transcribed in prose, resembles those works of poetry which are driven not by the dictates of outer realism - the world as we see it - but rather by the compulsions and fears of the world *behind* our eyes. The narrative can seem at times no more than a setting for images - grotesque, arresting, beautiful - thrown up by our desires or dreams. Two obvious examples are images of magical transformation, and the strange combinations of human and animal which run through most mythic traditions. Such myths offer a gateway into the worlds of symbol (a shape borrowed from the outer world but charged with inner meaning) and magic (the ability to abandon the laws of causality for the reign of supernatural order). The story of Blodeuwedd, in the fourth branch of *The Mabinogion,* is a tale driven by magical symbolism: its heroine is transformed from flower to woman, and her spouse, in the moment of death, becomes an eagle, and is then charmed into human form once more.

from The Writer's Workbook *eds. Jenny Newman, Aileen La Tourette and Edmund Cusick (Arnold 2000)*

***

Myth lives, and regenerates itself, by adaptation and reinterpretation. It is never so much told as retold. If for a long period it fails to be retold, it will inevitably lose its connection with generations who have grown up since it was first formulated, and will die into revered tradition or scholarly curiosity. Libraries are full of such dead myths, the preserved shells of an intuition no longer alive within any culture or audience, and thus no longer in a sense myths at all, but mere stories. It is through creative artists that the dead wood of myth may stir to life again, sprouting new shoots for each generation. This is most evident in the continual rediscovery of the metanarratives of religion, and, indeed, it would be possible to argue that all myth has, in its broadest sense, a spiritual element: it is, after all, concerned with apprehensions of what lies beyond conscious knowledge, such as the widely held belief in what we term fate. Myth may be bent to the purposes of moral instruction, but primarily it articulates or affirms our sense of our place in the universe: the way life is. The most obvious secular illustration of this process is the continuous reincarnation of the Arthurian cycle through poetry, fine art, novels, television and film to meet the changing needs of the societies which recreate it. *The Mabinogio*n offers another example: the high Gothic archaism of Lady Charlotte Guest's first English translation speaks the Victorians' language in more than a stylistic sense: it embodies the chivalric ethos through which so many Victorian struggles and ideals found expression.

It may be noted that the origins of *The Mabinogion* stories lie in oral traditions. Storytelling has never been mere recitation; it is, rather, the reimagining of a narrative in a way that becomes unique to each teller. The need for a partnership between imagination and memory, formerly the space within which the storyteller worked, but now also that of the poet, is evident from the text of *The Mabinogion*. Like other written records of oral traditions, the material of the Four Branches is sparse and laconic: a skeleton of plot awaiting the teller to flesh it out and breathe it into life. To a modern reader, used to texts intended as literature, *The Mabinogion* may seem curiously abbreviated and full of apparent gaps. Blodeuwedd's creation, life and demise are dealt with in a mere four pages. Furthermore, like Mallory's *Le Morte D'Arthur*, it is written in simple paratactic text; entirely, as it were, in the indicative mood: a bare chronicle of deeds. The realm of the subjunctive, of motivation and inner response, of the psychological meaning of the outward events to the characters, is left untouched, though the text still leaps into life in dialogue, in which a vibrant sense of character can burn through: *'Faith,' said she, 'thou wilt not go from me tonight.'*

***

The Story of Blodeuwedd

The tale of Blodeuwedd is best heard told. As a substitute, the story can be found in written form in the Fourth Branch of *The Mabinogion*. Here is a brief outline of the story.

A long time ago, there was in the Kingdom of Gwynedd a magician named Gwydion. Gwydion took a new born baby from its mother, Arianrhod, and adopted him. He was named Lleu Llaw Gyffes, which means 'skilful hand'. Arianrhod hated Gwydion because he had brought shame on her at the baby's birth, and in revenge laid a curse on her son, that no mortal woman would ever be his wife.

Gwydion and his Uncle, King Math, conspired to evade the spell, and create a wife for Lleu. She was indeed no mortal woman, for she was raised from Nature itself, being conjured by their arts from the spirits dwelling in the flowers of Oak, Broom and Meadowsweet, given shape in fleshly form. So well did they succeed in this that the work of their own hands was said to be the most beautiful and desirable woman ever seen in Gwynedd.

They named this woman Blodeuwedd, and she was wed to Lleu. King Math gave the couple Castle Mur to dwell in. One day when Lleu was absent, a huntsman named Gronw Pebyr came to the castle in pursuit of a stag, killing it beneath the walls. As it was late in the day, Blodeuwedd had her servants invite him in to eat with her. At table they looked on each other with love and desire, and that same night they lay together. In the morning Gronw was fearful of Lleu's return, and eager to be away, but such were Blodeuwedd's charms that she persuaded him to stay that night, and again another night. Before he left in the third dawn Blodeuwedd had hatched a plot to kill Lleu so that they could be together.

Killing Lleu was no easy matter, however, for Gwydion had placed charms upon him to protect his life: he might not be killed on land nor on water, indoors or outside, mounted or on foot. There was however one way in which these conditions might be fulfilled: if Lleu were to stand with one foot on the back of a billy goat, the other on the rim of a bath of water which was covered with a canopy. Even then he might not be killed unless it was with a spear that had been forged for a year, worked on only while all others were at mass. At once Blodeuwedd sent word to Gronw to begin forging just such a spear.

When the year was almost done Blodeuwedd told Lleu that she wished to keep him safe from harm, but that she could not protect his life unless she had a clearer image of how danger might threaten him. Thus she asked him to show her how he might be killed. Willing to obey her every whim, Lleu constructed on the slopes of Cwm Cynfal all that was needful for his death. When he stood beneath the canopy, with one foot in the bath and one on the back of the goat, Blodeuwedd cried to Gronw, who had concealed himself nearby, and Gronw cast the spear at Lleu, dealing the mortal blow. Lleu's soul gave a great cry and flew off in the form of an eagle.

Now that her husband had disappeared, Blodeuwedd brought Gronw to live with her in Castle Mur. Gwydion, however, devoted his life to searching for news of Lleu, and after many months he found him still in the form of an eagle, but one so injured that his flesh rotted and pigs fed on it. By magic and by poetry Gwydion brought Lleu back, and restored him to human form and to health.

Lleu told Gwydion what had been done to him, and they set off together to seek revenge. Blodeuwedd and Gronw heard of their approach and fled. Lleu caught up with Gronw and at Cwm Cynfael he made Gronw stand and receive a single spear cast as he himself had done. Gronw pleaded that as he had been led astray by a woman's wiles, he should be allowed a chance to live. Lleu granted him this wish and let him hide himself behind a stone, but so powerful was the spear-throw of Lleu of the skilful hand that it pierced the stone and cut through Gronw's heart also. A stone as tall as a man with a hole over the heart lies by the river Cynfael to this day.

Gwydion pursued Blodeuwedd, who fled with her maidens to a lake beyond Cym Cynfael, and running looking behind them they fell into the lake and drowned, all but Blodeuwedd, who, being immortal could not die. In punishment for her betrayal Gwydion turned her into an owl, a bird which every other bird shuns. Her voice is still heard at night, crying, and the name of the owl is flower-face to this day.

On Blodeuwedd

The Blodeuwedd story may hold warnings for women, as well as inspiration, but inspiration she has offered in abundance.

Blodeuwedd's attraction is unique. It is hard to think of a comparable figure about whom so many poets have written, even harder to think of one who continues to exert such imaginative appeal. This is the more remarkable when one considers that her mythos is derived from a tradition preserved from a pre-Christian oral tradition via an eight hundred year old text... It is worth remembering that Blodeuwedd is not the central character even of the written text in which she appears - from the point of view of the dynastic structure which underpins the plot of the Four Branches, she is a mere diversion. The Fourth Branch is pre-eminently the story of Gwydion. Pryderi's life has been the uniting strand of the first three Branches, and it is Gwydion who slays Pryderi. Blodeuwedd is no more than a minor player in this dynastic struggle. That Blodeuwedd should rise out of this marginalised position to seize her own identity may, however, be truer to her earliest origins than the written text of *The Mabinogion* may suggest. While I have neither the aim nor the qualifications to engage in historical or textual analysis of the myths which underlie *The Mabinogion,* there appears to be some evidence that Blodeuwedd may have had an existence independent to the story of Lleu Llaw Gyffes. In *The White Goddess* Robert Graves quotes other Blodeuwedd traditions. Indeed, Blodeuwedd may well have been a Goddess in her own right... She was the creation of Gwydion and Math, who were certainly of supernatural status. She was immortal... the wife of a God and was treated as an equal in the divine house of Math.

Comparative mythology would seem to indicate a greater importance for Blodeuwedd than simply as an extemporised device to evade the bride-curse cast by Arianrhod on Lleu... Blodeuwedd the flower-woman has a web of cognates and associations in nature deities such as Flora and Persephone which point to a wider significance. Blodeuwedd's name means, literally, 'in the image of a flower'...

To become engaged with the Blodeuwedd tradition, the imagination of the audience must be led into a world where supernatural events can be taken as an integral part of the cosmos, a shift that is made quite unconsciously when dealing with such areas of the fabulous as children's fairy tales.

Even without an academic investigation into the aetiology of the story, Blodeuwedd's nature points to other sources than those of the wars of Gwynedd and Dyfed. The common names of meadowsweet, 'Bridewort' and 'Queen of the Meadow', hint at its roots in the greenwood of faery, fertility, and nature spirits - the same dryadic realm that underlies the comedy of *A Midsummer Night's Dream*. Culpepper records Meadowsweet as a druidic plant. And *druid* is itself, it has been speculated, derived from the Welsh for oak, *derwen*. The oak is associated with woodland cults such as the English one of Herne the Hunter. Gronw is led by the hunt to find Blodeuwedd, just as another hunt leads Pwyll into the otherworld of Annwn. Graves notes broom, too, as one of the magical plants of the Celtic Tree Calendar.

Blodeuwedd's story makes other links through Western culture. The story of her creation, fall and punishment has inevitable resonance with the Genesis story of creation, expulsion and damnation. Gronw's exculpation 'since it was by a woman's wiles' echoes that of Adam 'the woman which you gave me...' Even closer to Blodeuwedd's story is that of Lilith, in Jewish lore Adam's first wife, punished by God for wishing to exercise her own position on sexual choice. Lilith is banished to the fringes of society, and of our knowledge. In the bible Lilith the *night hag* is diminished in translation becoming only *screech owl*. (Isaiah 13:21)

It is possible, at least, to conjecture that as elsewhere a text transcribed in a Christian age, by Christian scribes, distorts as it preserves vestiges of pre-Christian narratives. The life of the myth, as against its outward structure, is however not in its history but in the emotional meaning it bears. The 'poetic logic' ... is to see Blodeuwedd's owl incarnation, not as a punishment, but as a revelation of another aspect of her identity... The owl image is crucial here. Even within British folklore, behind the homely image of the wise old owl lie older associations with Witchcraft. As its Latin name - *Strix Minerva* - reminds us, the owl is the symbol of the Goddesses Athena and Hecate.

The unity that Blodeuwedd offers between paradoxical images: the passive, beautiful flower, and the nocturnal hunter, the unnerving combination of Flora and Hecate, may explain some of her appeal for poets, for poetry thrives in imaginative tension and in paradox... The elements of the natural world from which she is incarnated may offer further grounds for her attraction. The owl, the oak, meadowsweet and broom are still physically present in our landscape: still close enough to us to provoke new encounters. It is difficult in formal, academic prose to cite subjective experiences as in any way evidential for the reader, who may be coming to Blodeuwedd's myth for the first time. It is harder still to convey, from the overcrowded world of the word processor, electric light and traffic noise, a sense of a figure whose provenance is quintessentially solitary, nocturnal and rural.

Blodeuwedd's origins are poetical in another sense. While Math and Gwydion share in Blodeuwedd's creation it is Gwydion who carries forward the momentum of the action. ...Gwydion is 'the best teller of tales in the world' and in a time of oral culture it is a short step from storyteller to poet, literally, of course, a 'maker'. If there are truths about women's experience in the myth of Blodeuwedd, there are, equally, truths for the creative artist hidden in the 'parent' story of Gwydion, the man who makes Blodeuwedd. Blodeuwedd does seem to bear some mark of her creator. Gwydion's own paradoxical flashes of cunning, ruthlessness, lust and loyalty to those he loves dominate and fascinate throughout the Fourth Branch. But if Blodeuwedd is Gwydion's poem, then she is one who reverts under his hand, as poems will, becoming her own thing. ...

Gwydion's creation of a woman takes poetic creation into a new dimension. As the poet compared his love to a rose, so poetic language allows, for example, the figure of speech in which the scent of meadowsweet can symbolise sensual allure. Gwydion's creation, however, transcends that of language: his words become flesh, metaphor becoming magic, making the woman herself. Like a poem, Blodeuwedd is woven from symbols. Those creative artists who follow him respond to the same symbols in a new act of creation. ...

The 'imagery' of poetry shares a linguistic root with 'magic' and with 'imagination'. Gwydion's sorcery offers the poet a seductive paradigm of taking the art of making beyond words. What he can 'conjure' are not merely images in the mind of the hearer but physical realities. ...

To our own age, acutely sensitised to gender politics, Blodeuwedd offers one complex example of the interrelationships of power and sex... Blodeuwedd's creation is indeed a response to male desire. But having been created, her story is one of domination of the men around her: the seduction and control of Gronw (who struggles, but fails, to leave her), the manipulation of Lleu, and the stage-managing of her husband's murder. She is commanding, daring, ingenious, and patient... Husband and lover both obey her unquestioningly unto death. Gronw's disclaimer 'it was through a woman's wiles' may seem to be a typically male attempt to shift responsibility, but it could equally be read as the testimony of an ordinary mortal matched against extraordinary charisma or supernatural power. Blodeuwedd remains strong till the end: only her creator can oppose her and even he, it seems, cannot destroy her.

Blodeuwedd's banishment can be seen as emblematic of the silencing of the female voice in a patriarchal culture - banished beyond the pale and robbed, like Philomel, of the power of speech. But the owl, of all birds, is not silenced: its voice lingers, haunting and unmistakable. And Blodeuwedd's apparent punishment offers a power that the flower maiden never had: woman reborn as predator, as huntress. ...

Once again Blodeuwedd has a multivalent quality. She can be seen to play more than one role in the sex war. She is victim: shaped, exploited and eventually punished by men. She is scarlet woman, seductive, rebellious, and dominating. She is vengeful crone, or the voice of wisdom in the woods. As Jung makes clear, one of the characteristics of symbolic or archetypal figures is that they can bear a number of conflicting meanings. One thing is plain in all these versions from her meeting with Gronw: she is an intensely sexual creature.

Myth is patient, and waits for each generation to hear it, waits, too, to be spoken. It has been suggested elsewhere that *The Mabinogion* is full of powerful women, to such an extent that it might have been written by a woman. On the evidence of the Four Branches, any woman with power would seem to be met with traumatic punishment: rape, kidnap, public or private humiliation. There are other sorts of power, however. Blodeuwedd has the power to inspire, the power to work within the imagination. Her triumphs and sufferings offer a symbolic set of experiences which, through a poet's eye, may serve as symbols for aspects of the lives of contemporary women... Blodeuwedd is more symbol than role model. It is the complex facets of her nature that exercise the imagination ... The central drama of her life, the seduction of Gronw and love, intrigue, betrayal, and murder, receive less attention than do her incarnation and transformations: flower, woman, owl. She is, perhaps, functioning not so much as an individual with a fictional biography as a symbolic persona into whom poets step, a contemporary example of the Yeatsian poetic mask.

In one sense, of course, Blodeuwedd is and remains near. The chronological origins of her story may be disputed, but it is tied to definite places. Lleu's name appears in place names across the landscape of modern Gwynedd. Caer Daethyl, Castell Mur and Cwm Cynfael, named as the sites of Blodeuwedd's creation, life, and transformation, are though remote and overgrown, accessible to this day. These signs are public, available to all. But for the individual, Blodeuwedd - symbol, myth, presence - may herself appear for a moment to brush the surface of daily life. ...

Blodeuwedd's presence may be felt in subtle ways, a Goddess banished from recognition by patriarchal ordinance, but still capable of gleaming into life for individuals in those moments when spiritual intuition touches the imagination...

from the introduction to Blodeuwedd: An Anthology of Women's Poetry, *edited by Edmund Cusick (Headland, 2001)*

Gronw's Stone: Voices from the Mabinogion (1997)

Introduction

I first met Edmund 13 years ago, on a story telling course at Ty Newydd, the National Writers' Centre in North Wales, during which we visited historic sites and learned the stories of *The Mabinogion*. My memory is that we were both unwell, I had the tail end of shingles, he had a horiible cold and was living on Lem-sip and chocolate. The week was magical. Our group of five became good friends, listening to each other's stories, both those we were trying to learn and our own private ones.

Before we parted, we made promises to meet again. As we had been told was customary amongst storytellers, we each, in turn, made a boast of what we would do before we met again. I boasted that I would write a poem for each of the women in *The Mabinogion*.

Next Spring we met again at Avebury and told stories amongst the stones. Edmund confessed that he had written a poem for Pwyll, Prince of Dyfed. As he read it, it became clear that Edmund's Pwyll was an honourable man, above reproach, almost holy, a knight of the round table. I was upset. I pointed out to him that Pwyll was not totally wonderful, he knew that the Queen of Annwn thought him to be her husband, he knew that she longed for his tenderness at night, he knew how much his turning from her caused her pain. As we argued this back and forth, I started to write her reply. I wrote into the night, reading aloud to Edmund at every pause for breath. Edmund later changed the tone of his poem to include Pwyll's gentle regret. This is how it started: *Gronw's Stone*.

We lived in the stories, in each other's work. Edmund wrote poems in the male voices and I in the female voices. We edited and revised together. When we were asked, but you don't say who wrote which poems in the book, we honestly replied that it had not occurred to us to do so. I would know a poem of Edmund's anywhere, even if it were found in an attic years from now. He would have said the same of mine.

And so began a creative partnership that didn't end, we continued to share almost everything we wrote. He was astonished at my clarity, I was taken aback by the gentle beauty of his language, how slowly and carefully he chose it. We had an understanding of each other's thinking beyond the words.

Ann Gray

A selection from Gronw's Stone

The First Branch

Pwyll, Prince of Dyfed, hunted in the forests of Arberth. At the end of the day his hounds picked up the scent of a great stag, and brought it to bay in the woods of Glyn Cuch. As Pwyll approached he saw another pack around the stag, each hound of which was pure white. No sooner had he driven them off than Arawn, King of Annwn, the Otherworld, appeared, whose hounds they were. To amend the dishonour he had done to the King, Pwyll agreed to do anything he should ask of him. The King requested that Pwyll change places with him for a year and a day. At the end of that year Pwyll should fight a duel with Hafgan, whose lands in Annwn bordered Arawn's.

During his year in Annwn, all that the King had, his hall, his men, his hounds and his horses, would belong to Pwyll, even his wife. The enchantment was such that none was aware of the deception. Pwyll ruled Annwn well, but although he could conduct himself tenderly by day, he found his honour forbade him to touch the Queen at night. When the year ended Pwyll fought and killed Hafgan, and returned to Dyfed.

One day he rode to the enchanted hill of Gorsedd Arberth. Here, it was said, if any dared to stand upon it he would either see a great marvel or suffer grievous blows. It was here he first caught sight of Rhiannon, riding on a white horse, whom he later married. After they had been married for several years Rhiannon gave birth to a son. Six serving women were ordered to keep watch over mother and child, but failed to do so. During the night the child vanished. Fearful of punishment, the women pretended Rhiannon herself had destroyed her child in a fit of madness after childbirth. They killed newborn puppies from her hounds, smeared Rhiannon's face and hands with blood, and scattered bones among the bedclothes. Rhiannon was found guilty. Her punishment was to wait for seven years outside the gates, telling strangers her story and offering to carry them on her back into the city. After several years a series of magical events, and the loyalty of Teyrnon and his wife, restored her child, Pryderi, to her.

Pwyll

Nothing may I take from you
whom I have lain by for a year,
not even your leave.
Behind my eyelids I see ivory hounds
gleaming around the stag I brought to bay,
my own dogs shivering.
That night I first came to you,
dressed in your husband's flesh,
your skin was blue-white as his hounds, your body
wet as snow for me, your touch eager, burning
like ice that steals the blood heat from the mouth.
Something held me back, though you were willing,
that night, and each night since. It was not fear,
nor yet honour for he whose place I took.
I wished, perhaps, to keep some deed untrespassed;
desiring, but not wanting, this last communion;
knowing I would care for no mortal woman
after you. And it is so.
You do not know me, trapped
behind your master's eyes,
guess only disdain as I turn my face to the wall.
Each night, I hear desire
and pride wrestle in your breathing;
after that, despair.
The sun's warmth strokes your hair,
embraces you. Before night falls
I will hunger for you,
wish I had been
less pure.

The Second Branch

Branwen, daughter of the Welsh King, Bran, was married to the King of Ireland in a bid to unite the two countries. When he heard of this, her half-brother Efnysien savagely maimed the Irish King's horses. Later, at the Irish court, the memory of this was revived, and Branwen, who had given birth to a son, Gwern, was punished. She was imprisoned in the kitchens and brutalised daily. Eventually her father came to her rescue, and raised war to avenge the insults that had been paid to her. In the chaos that followed she was forced to watch her own son being burned to death by Efnysien. Bran himself was wounded in the foot by a poisoned spear. Before the poison could work through his body, he commanded that his own head be struck off, so that he could continue to speak to his companions after his death. With Bran's severed head the seven warriors who alone had survived the conflict returned at last to Harlech. There Branwen died, and there they began a feast. It is said that whilst they ate, the birds of Rhiannon, who can charm the living and wake the dead, came to them. Seven years passed.

Manawydan

I remember only a castle
high by the sea, snow driving,
hissing in the grate. Then stones
baking in the summer heat, the swift
flicker of the leaves' turning
as we passed the flagon. They say
we told tales for seven years. There were
tales we did not tell: the stink
of the heaped dead, the din
of crows, the cold couplings
of the slain, the song a baby sings,
burning. Branwen's white hand
we could not cover, pointing
stiff through the thin soil, the grate
of a blunted sword in bone.

The Third Branch

After many adventures, Pryderi and Manawydan returned to Wales, where Manawydan married Rhiannon, Pwyll's widow and Pryderi's mother. Together Pryderi, his wife Cigfa, Manawydan and Rhiannon rode to the hill of Gorsedd Arberth. On the hill top, a violent storm broke, and when the darkness cleared, they found themselves in a country full of a marvellous light, but empty of people. While hunting in this country the dogs of Pryderi and Manawydan flushed out a white boar. Pryderi followed it, and found himself in a Caer, or castle, where there had been none before. He entered it, but did not return. When Manawydan reported news of his loss to Rhiannon, Rhiannon followed Pryderi into the Caer. Neither returned, and, with a peal of thunder, the Caer disappeared. Cigfa was left alone with Manawydan. After many adventures, Manawydan succeeded in restoring Rhiannon and Pryderi from the enchantment which had been placed upon them.

Pryderi at the Caer

In magic was I born and will I die.
At Gorsedd Arberth I saw my fate
revealed. There was no death there,
in that other country
that dawned through the mist.
That world we found,
the image of our own, shot through
with light; the stones glittering: jade, serpentine,
emerald. It lies there always,
perhaps, within our hills, our souls'
sight too gross to glimpse it.
At its heart, I found a Caer
traced in brittle ice, its gates
frozen into pearl, an altar in
a pool of radiance, a scarlet
chalice. When I touched it, flame
sprang in four swift tongues
piercing my palms, streaming
into heaven, till I cried out, my heart burning
to its metre. And I beheld Gorsedd
Arberth and Golgotha, Caer Sidi
and Jerusalem, Eden and Annwn
bound through this place,
as in the frost the web
binds branch to branch: the stone
raised at Felinrhyd, the stars'
cold dance above Maen Tyryawg.

The Fourth Branch

When Math, King of Gwynedd, was not at war, he rested his feet in the lap of a maiden. Her name was Goewin. Math had two nephews: Gwydion and Gilfaethwy. Gilfaethwy conceived a violent passion for Goewin. As Math was a magician, and could hear every word whispered on the wind, Gilfaethwy told no one. Gwydion his brother was a sorcerer, and resolved to help him. By cheating Pryderi, Gwydion started a war with the Kingdom of Dyfed, Math left his court and Goewin unprotected. Together Gwydion and Gilfaethwy raped Goewin, then joined the war in which, with the aid of magic, Gwydion killed Pryderi at Felinrhyd. He was buried at Maen Tyryawg.

When Math returned from war, Goewin told him what had been done to her. Math married her and punished his nephews, transforming them first into a hind and a stag; then a boar and sow; then a wolf and a she wolf. Each transformation lasted for a year and in each they produced offspring together: a fawn, a young boar, and a wolf-cub. Then, forgiven, the two brothers were returned to human form.

In search of another lap maiden, Math turned to Gwydion for advice. He suggested Arianrhod, his sister. To test her virginity, Arianrhod had to step over a golden wand, but as she did so, two infants fell from her womb. The first ran to the sea and never returned. The second was seen only by Gwydion, who wrapped it in silk and concealed it in a chest in his room. This child grew to be Lleu, whom Gwydion loved as his own son. Arianrhod, furious with Gwydion, cursed the child that he would have no wife born of mortal woman.

To evade the curse and find Lleu a wife, Math and Gwydion resorted to magic, and conjured a bride from trees and herbs. They named her Blodeuwedd. The tale of the creation of a beautiful woman by the dark arts was retold so often that Blodeuwedd's fame spread far beyond Gwynedd. Alone at court, her husband away hunting, Blodeuwedd heard hunters nearby and instructed her men to offer them hospitality overnight. She met Gronw Pebyr, Lord of Penllyn, and they became lovers. Despite his anxiety lest Lleu should return, Gronw Pebyr stayed with her for three nights. Blodeuwedd, now determined to kill her husband so that she might be with Gronw, won from Lleu the secret of the charm set on his life. He could only be slain by a spear whose head was forged while all others were at mass. Gronw made the spear and killed Lleu, but his spirit stayed on earth in the form of an eagle, to be restored to human form by Gwydion. Gwydion then punished Blodeuwedd by transforming her into an owl. Gronw, challenged by Lleu, agreed to stand in the place where Lleu had himself received Gronw's spear-cast, to receive one blow from him. Before the blow could be struck, Gronw hid behind a huge slab of rock. Lleu's spear pierced the rock and killed him.

A stone as tall as a man, with a hole over the heart, lies by the river Cynfael to this day.

Gronw

The forge grows hot, demanding
me again. The last sabbath
of a year of sabbaths.
I did not seek
this fate, nor did I
deny it. Blame the stars,
Gronw, or the beast
that led you to her gate.
Its blood not washed
from off me, before she gave
the kiss of greeting. Her dogs,
mine, coupling outside the walls.
And within, Lleu's hall,
strewn with mint and vervain.
Blodeuwedd. You gave me honeycomb
from your hives, broke it
with white fingers, pressed
sweetness to my lips, while
the trembling harpist sang
of another hunt, another Lord's
wife. Your eyes devoured me
as if there were no shame
nor ever had been in that hall.
When I rose
your small fists drew my mouth

to yours, as a child, mad of thirst,
pulls brambles to it
careless of the thorns, brought me
to your bed. And as I entered
you I closed my eyes, drowning
in the breath of honeysuckle
piled by that tall bed
and after, opened them, saw
the slow bees within, clad
in cloying pollen, wings gummed
with nectar, fumbling
in torpor, and I slept.
The iron glows. While you
and he eat Christ's
flesh I labour here. I see
your eyes watching; flickering
in the reeds, the leaves,
impatient. A final stroke.
Here is the spear
to pierce his side.

A short story
VIVIEN

"This one's for you, Vivien," said Nigel, emerging from his office. Then, standing closer than I'd have liked, "Christ, you look hot. Everyone else wears T-shirts, you know. I assure you, my dear, I wouldn't mind seeing more of you."

I ignored the leer and opened it, a standard folder embossed, as usual, with our logo: the words *Millennium Heritage Trust* in gold, and a tower illuminated by a rising sun. Inside was a photocopy from the property pages of August's *Country Life*.

Island Dream

Private Island, thirty acres, 150 miles South West of Penzance. Period house (2 bedrooms), various outbuildings, own harbour. This unique property is of historic significance and unparalleled character.

Underneath, in his executive red ink, he'd written

Status: Priority Purchase
Surveyor: Vivien Hughes

"You're joking," I said, as the door closed. My first survey. I should be excited, flattered, I knew. But that was what worried me. Why me? I'd only just been hired to do a bit of valuation. My background was fine art: I knew nothing about land. And I also knew damn well we wouldn't put a Priority Purchase on the Tower of London before the survey had been done. I steeled myself, called Nigel's extension. He was as smooth as ever.

"Of course I'm serious, Vivien. It's one of our obligations under the charter - preserve and protect, you know. Take your time over it, my dear."

It takes either a very good liar, or someone who's been lied to very well, to spot another. I qualified on both accounts. If it had been legit, Nigel wouldn't have bothered being condescending, he'd just have told me to do my bloody job and be grateful. A scam of some sorts. I turned my face to the fan. God, it was hot.

Of course. August. In three weeks time the accounts would be closed for the year, as the season ended. The annual audit. I'd already wondered how we were going to cope with an embarrassing surplus in one of our current accounts. If HM treasurer should ever work out, as I had in a couple of months, that The Millennium Heritage Trust was not so much preserving and protecting the Nation's Property as dealing in it for profit then Nigel would find himself out of a job. Or worse.

We needed to buy something now, quickly, to get rid of the money. Purchasing ahead of survey was unheard of, but the sale would go through, our capital balance go down, and then, a month later, my survey would point out how mad the whole idea was, and he'd sell it. Take your time, he'd said. And then the money would find its way to one of Nigel's other little accounts. That was why he'd given it to me: hopelessly unqualified, unlikely to ask questions. And, if it came to it, easily overruled. I phoned him back, assumed the girly sycophancy he liked.

"Do some background work? Certainly, Vivien, we want a really thorough job. I'll authorise an account for you. Good-bye, my dear."

That simple. A week's paid leave. Expenses. Cornwall.

I wasn't extravagant. A decent business hotel, no wine on the bill, and I started work. A small donation from the trust account to the local antiquarian society, together with some professional flirting and some legally worthless hints of a larger donation to the county library, yielded a pile of documents I had no right to, and I retired to my room. After two days I had boiled it all down to three paragraphs.

Inys Morgen

Island formed of two granite outcrops, rising to 55m., situated 35.15 West, 40.28 North. Accessible by boat, from Penzance (8 hours) or St. Lyon (6 hours).

History: tradition holds Inys Morgen as the site of Celtic hermitage, variously dedicated to a number of female saints. Considered uninhabitable till, in 1884, an archaeological excavation, undertaken by The British and Cornish Archaeological Association, led by Thomas Trehearne, found evidence of fifth and sixth century habitation.

In 1887 Trehearne purchased the island and constructed the current house and harbour. After Trehearne's death in 1903 the island was bequeathed to the British and Cornish Archaeological Association. Requisitioned in 1940 for use as a long range navigation station for Coastal Command. Retained by the Ministry of Defence until Defence Review of 1999, when recommended for sale.

It was okay for Nigel but it left out the interesting bits. It didn't mention the peculiarities of the Reverend Enoch Trehearne, priest of the Church of England, father of eleven children, Freemason and founder member of the Hermetic Order of the Golden Dawn. From his long, gaunt face, the hollow eyes sunk in their sockets stared out at me from a hundred-year old photograph. Also gracing my desk was his masterwork, *Cornish Saints and the Arthurian Tradition*, a mixture of church history, legend, and lunacy. Then there was the British and Cornish Archaeological Association, responsible for financing the dig and then, bizarrely, the construction of new buildings on top of their prime site. Its benefactors, with modest unanimity, were anonymous. Its proceedings were unavailable, its accounts in private hands. Old Enoch could have taught Nigel a thing or two about organised fraud. I had to admire him.

The Sea Queen, out of Penzance, stank of cod and diesel. We sailed with the tide into the scarlet remains of sunset. The skipper took my money but refused all attempts of communication. It was a rough crossing. Rain came, and seasickness. I clung to the rail in the darkness. I had developed asthma in my teens and now it was a torment, breathing hard through heavy spray and sea-mist. Sleep was impossible and now I faced the devil's hours alone. 3 a.m. The hour the lies run thin, the hour not to be awake. The hour my parents had been killed, my father driving too late, too tired, they'd told me, and, I found out later, after one or two for the road. The hour I'd made my first attempt so that now I had to keep my wrists hidden, whatever Nigel liked. The hour I'd given up any hope of becoming an artist, acknowledging, at last, my lack of talent. Art had been my only religion, and that night I knew I had failed in it. Alone and shivering, I saw my life fall apart before my eyes, the past and then the future. I saw where it would end, the scams, the frauds, the plans getting more and more tangled and, through it all, my self-hatred growing, the sense of chances running out.

It was then the water invited me. It would be swift. No more pain, just rest. I seized the rail, brought my weight up. But, with a gut-wrenching lurch, the boat pitched high, throwing me back onto the deck. I landed heavily on one knee, twisting it, and cried aloud. The sea, too, rejected me, and my courage failed.

With infinite slowness, the darkness thinned, and the fog grew from grey to white. The engine note changed. Then, out of the mist, a wall of rock, and, a minute later, a tiny harbour. For a man who had claimed no knowledge of the place, the skipper seemed to have a fine eye for navigating blind. A jetty of decaying concrete, draped in seaweed, reached out to us. Nauseous and shivering, I jumped, slipped, fell on the same knee I had hurt before, cursed with pain. The skipper watched, unmoved.

"Eight hours," he shouted.

I clung to the wet weed. A swish of wake, and he was gone. Cold. The slap on sea rock. A path led up into the mist. I climbed unsteadily, limping. Each step brought pain. After a few precarious minutes, the path divided. Which way? I took the left hand fork, a thread of darkness in the white blur of mist. I climbed again, and saw the dark silhouette of a building. The house? I hobbled around it. A door. It pushed open, closed behind me under its own weight. Even breathing, in this damp, was hard. In pitch darkness I stepped forward and collided into something. My knee cracked against hard wood in front of me. It was then, spurred by the pain, that I slipped to the stone floor and started to cry.

When it was over, I felt the warm blood on my hands, the shattered dial of my watch, cuts among the bruises. I had been beating my fists on the wood in front of me. Perhaps, if I was lucky, I would die here in the dark. My breathing was easier, as though some subtle change had passed through the air. I opened my eyes. Out of the gloom, a raw wound of colour was bleeding light: dancing in reds and greens. I stood up, and I knew where I was. I was in a chapel. Ahead of me was my salvation. A stained glass window.

The background was of brilliant emerald. Interlacing branches of green and black reached to the edge of the frame and on them were tiny flowers of pink and white. Three female figures stood tall enough to fill the frame. Their hair, gold, black and auburn by turns, fell to their waists, and each bore a circlet of silver. They wore garments that fell from breast to ankle, each of one colour, scarlet, blue, violet. Each, in medieval style, bore a token: she to the right, fair-haired, bore a wedge of golden honeycomb, and she to the left, whose hair was auburn, a single scarlet apple. The lady in the centre had a crown on her black hair. She bore a silver chalice. A trinity. I walked towards it, hesitated. I felt a strange sensation, a rushing wave as of cold air around me that settled in a knot of liquid cold in each palm as though I held melting ice in my hands. Slowly I approached the altar. I made out a decanter of dark wine. I lifted the cold weight of the stopper, dipped my finger, tasted, smiled with surprise. I looked up. The Queen looked back at me with slanted, violet eyes. The mouth was cold. Whatever - whoever - was represented there was not human. A fairy queen or demoness? There was apple blossom behind her but this was not Eden. I looked again behind the offered apple in the left hand panel. There was no coiled snake. No sin. Only honey. This was a pagan fruit - the apple of the Otherworld. What did they call it? Avalon. The Isle of Avalon. Paradise. The sea boomed again. A single drop of golden honey seemed to drip from one finger, glowing like amber.

It was a Burne-Jones. There was no mistaking it. The Quest of the Sangraal series. And this one was unknown, the fulfilment of them all. God. It would be a nine-day sensation. A lost masterpiece discovered on the furthest flung piece of England. The M.o.D. would look pretty silly. Hadn't the RAF ever looked in here? Of course. Various outbuildings. To them, it would just be another piece of church glass. The last Burne-Jones in a lost chapel in the sea. The Art press would go berserk and, after them, the Quality Sundays. The whole island would become a national treasure. Nigel would make a killing.

If I told him.

It wouldn't be hard. I still knew people from College - the successful ones - people who knew people. A trip to London. A deal. After my report, the trust would sell the whole island and a gallery could buy it through some innocuous third party. And, in return, I could name my price. Not money. A job - something I believed in. Valuation, perhaps, or my own gallery. I was looking at my salvation. All this passed through my mind in seconds.

I tore myself away. Outside, my eyes were dazzled by the sun. The mist had gone and I saw the island laid out beneath me, bare as another St Kilda. I stood on the shoulder of one of the two rocky crests. Beneath, in the waist of low land between them, lay the house and, below it, the harbour. Still half-blind in the glare, I saw a tangled spiral of barbed wire gleaming like a spider's web in steel. The incongruity of war in such a place. I felt, somehow, immeasurable relief, lightness, to be here, now. My knee seemed better. A little unsteadily, I walked down to the house. It had stood up well to the Atlantic gales though there were tiles missing, paint peeling. A wooden door. I pushed through it, to a kitchen. A squat black stove. A whisky bottle on the windowsill, the cap unbroken. A table with a tea-pot, two clean cups. There was a man sitting in an ancient arm chair. There was something about his long, thin features that seemed familiar, and for a moment another picture flashed into my mind. His eyes were closed. As I looked, unbelieving, they opened, regarding me as though half-focused.

"Would you like a cup of tea?"

I had almost screamed but he had stayed seated and that reassured me. He was offering me a cup of tea. Then I saw his hands tremble. Christ, he was more frightened than I was. But the voice, the eyes, were kind, if troubled. My instinct told me he was not dangerous. Probably. I relaxed a fraction.

"Sorry to startle you," he said. "I was…um asleep."

He was not a good liar which, in its way, reassured me, whatever he had been doing. The voice was gentle, the accent somewhere between Truro and Sloane Square. So were the clothes: tweed jacket, heavy boots, faded cord trousers, a check shirt.

"Why didn't you let me know there was someone here? You must have heard the bloody boat!"

"Yes. But I thought you'd come here straight away. That's why I made you some tea." - he gestured to the table - "but I hadn't reckoned on the mist. You went the other way, up to the chapel, I didn't want to…to disturb you there."

But it was the chapel, not me, I sensed, which needed to be left undisturbed.

"Yes," I said. "It's quite a place."

"Indeed, Miss Hughes."

I tensed.

"Sorry. Penzance is a small place. You're Vivien Hughes, aren't you, from the Millennium Heritage Trust? We heard you were coming out here."

"Oh? We being…"

"The British and Cornish Archaeological Association. I expect you've heard of us if you've been looking into the island's history."

"Yes. The Reverend Trehearne. But only until 1940. Are you telling me you're still going?"

"That's right."

"And now the M.o.D. is selling the place, you're trying to come back?"

"Not exactly. The thing is, we never really left."

"Never?"

"Well, during the war, of course. But even then the place was never garrisoned. They never built their radar, in the end."

Something about his assurance irritated me.

"Is the Ministry of Defence aware that you're in illegal occupation of restricted crown property?"

"No. But I doubt they'd mind, now."

"We might, though. You know we have certain special privileges, Mr…"

"Simon'll do."

"Well, Simon, under our charter we can put a compulsory purchase order on this place if we feel its heritage value is under threat. Neat, isn't it? So the…um…Association might find itself without a home."

I knew I'd scored then, but he seemed to keep his cool.

"Quite. Quite so. That's why you're here. And will you buy it?"

"Yes. I'm here to survey it."

His hands shook slightly, I saw, and he pushed them into his pockets.

"Oh."

Neither of us spoke. Through the door behind me I could hear the swell breaking on the rocks. Of course, *The Sea Queen* would have brought him here. Perhaps other boats, too. They would be well paid for keeping quiet. And for bringing supplies in, too, presumably.

We both let the silence linger. Then curiosity overcame me. The Burne-Jones. *The Sleep of Arthur in Avalon* ... the one the world thought he had died painting, giving the last of his strength to it.

"That window? It's uncatalogued. Was it the last thing he designed?"

"It was a private gift."

"A private…? God, you're not saying he was in your association - Avalon, the works?"

"He was very interested in the Arthurian tradition," he said, choosing his words. Then, as though quoting, "I am at Avalon, not yet in Avalon…"

Once again his condescension infuriated me.

"I know the line. Letter to Georgiana, the summer before he died."

"You're an expert?"

"It's what I'm paid for."

I paused, letting things click together.

"So you really believe this place is Avalon? That's what Trehearne was on about, underneath it all? This lump of rock? You're mad."

He was quiet for so long that I began to listen again to the sea, rising and breaking, falling and rising against the shore. When he spoke, I barely heard him at first.

"The dig we did in 1884 - you know about it?"

I nodded.

"There were a lot of pieces of fine glass. Apothecaries' phials. A pestle, parts of a mortar. It was a place of healing. And it was a shrine, we know that, don't ask me how. All this is Fifth, Sixth Century. If a king - Arthur, say - was wounded and the mainland was over-run, this would have been the obvious place to bring him."

"But Avalon? It's only a myth."

"Better for people to think that, if the king was here."

"But Paradise - the Isle of Apples?"

"The sea level's risen since the sixth century. Most of the old island is under the sea. As for apples, the Romans had vines in Cornwall, - apricots, even. It was warmer then. We know they had an orchard here."

His sureness irritated me, as did the well-rehearsed lunacy.

"So your Association came across one of the most important Dark Age sites in Britain and published a pack of lies? Some nonsense about a minor Celtic hermitage?"

"The secret - the dig, that is - had come to us in a special way. We wanted to keep it special. The Association has - had - other interests."

"I know." My mind leaped to Enoch's biography. The Order of the Golden Dawn. It was still going on.

"You're all into the occult, aren't you?"

For the first time I knew I had the advantage. His face went blank with surprise.

"Yes, if you want to put it like that. Magic is probably an easier word. Less Gothic Horror, as it were."

I looked at the old tweed, the sad, hollow hazel eyes, the tea pot. The nervous hands.

"Don't worry. I can't exactly see you sacrificing black cockerels under a full moon."

He kept a straight face. "Oh, I don't know…now and again."

We laughed then, together, the only time, and his thin, elongated face looked years younger. I found it hard to stop laughing: the delayed shock of the meeting, all that had happened in the chapel, the tension between us, all releasing. Not that I trusted him. But we drank tea, in Avalon. He was younger than he looked, only thirty. Had been a land agent in Devon. Before that, once, an engraver, but had given it up. Now he was the guardian of the island, whatever that meant. He knew something about art. Less than me.

"So do you have rituals here?"

He seemed to choose his words. “We have meditations.”

“What for?”

“You’d laugh, Miss Hughes.”

“Probably. Tell me anyway.”

“For Britain, for its spiritual welfare.”

“If you’ve been doing them since the 1880s, they don’t seem to have done much good.”

“Oh I don’t know. They brought you out here.”

Was this flirting? It seemed out of character.

“That’s very flattering but I was sent by my boss. On the off-chance that we might turn the place into a theme park - the Hermitage experience, perhaps.”

I looked out of the window to where a line of turquoise waves was curving like a lens of glass, holding the rock for a second in its reflection.

“God, if Nigel knew what you’d told me. The genuine Avalon. He’d rebuild it from scratch. Teenagers on youth training schemes in plastic armour. Fibreglass battlements. Wenches. All cleavage and mulled wine. It’d make Tintagel look like the British Museum.”

I stopped, suddenly angry. “Why did you tell me? I can tell them all this, you know. Or get the place excavated again. Christ, you know we were about to buy it! Why trust me?”

“Because of what happened in the chapel.”

“How do you know what happened in there?”

Now he was quiet again, almost grave.

“How long were you in there?”

I looked down. The watch was broken, of course, all jagged glass. I looked outside at the sun. It seemed higher, somehow, than it should have been.

“Half an hour? Three quarters? What’s that got to - ”

“Four and a half hours?”

“No.”

I stood up and went to the window. Had I passed out? I must have. Had he heard me screaming? It would seem not. God, what a mess.

“So will you tell them?” he asked.

“Avalon? No, I won’t tell them. We’ve destroyed enough places as it is.”

“Thank you, Miss Hughes.”

Why did he have to thank me? My own plan, the trip to London, the gallery. That deal would tear this place apart, just as effectively, though less obviously. They'd rip out the window and ship it back to London. Or they'd turn this place into an offshore St. Ives. Cultural Tourism. Guide books instead of candy floss. Either way, his island, their island, would disappear. A century of peace here, of the chapel, their crazy rituals. And I would destroy it. I knew. I had to.

"Let me show you the island?"

"Okay."

Outside the sun was hot. We climbed to the other tiny summit, looked over to the chapel. All around the sea held us, enchanted. The sun, the wind were intoxicating and I rolled up my sleeves, stopped. His eyes flicked down, then looked away. I hated him then, hating him and the red scars on my white flesh equally. I would destroy them both, destroy him, and the past. I knew that. I would do it. He was still looking away while I fumbled with my cuffs.

"Did you read the inscription in the chapel?" he asked, not looking at me.

"I didn't see one."

"'For him who finds me, I shall heal all wounds.'"

I was fighting more tears now, furious at his pity.

"Healed you then, has it? Or are you still drying out?"

His shoulders flinched.

Neither of us spoke.

Then he asked, "Is it that obvious?"

"I notice things. There's grape juice in the chapel instead of communion wine. The whisky in the kitchen - that's a kind of test, isn't it? And who gives up engraving to be a land agent, for God's sake!. You lost it all."

"Yes."

"And don't expect me to be sorry. I've had enough from liars. And drunks. My father, amongst others."

We were silent again, for a long time. Each listening to the sea; and not listening.

"So all this business about the Association. Aren't they a bit crazy to let you look after this place? If it's so important?"

He was angry now, which was what I wanted, I think. To smash through the charm, the pretence. But he kept his voice almost calm.

"'For him who finds me' - there's a tradition that the keeper of the island is someone who has some injury, some wound. Our founder - Trehearne. He had TB. But this place kept him alive, cured him. This is my wound, in a way. And - I'm trusted."

"And being a descendant of the great man helps, I suppose?"

"God. Where do you come from?" Again his voice was shocked. I was almost satisfied.

"The big world. I've had his photo on my desk for the last week. There's a resemblance. I've also read his correspondence."

"How did you get hold of that?" The anger was barely controlled now.

"The usual. Flirting. Money."

Far away, a faint stuttering sounded on the air. I looked at my watch, useless. Eight hours? It could not be. But perhaps, here, it could. *The Sea Queen* was in sight, a white flicker of bow-wave, the square cabin.

"I'm going."

"Yes," he said.

We looked at each other, the two of us half-sick with anger, hatred. I walked away, and he followed. The sound of the engine echoed off the concrete jetty. The skipper raised his hand in a gesture that was more salute than greeting. Suddenly the whole thing seemed wrong. All of it. And it already seemed half-real. The chapel, this man alone in his hermitage, the violence of my attack, the need to destroy him. I did not understand.

The wake splashed against the quay and an unfriendly hand reached out to grab me aboard. This was wrong, all wrong. I turned back and, without warning, he kissed me. Not with affection, still less with desire. I cannot describe that kiss - his lips pressed on mine for barely a second; chaste, detached. Neither forgiveness nor anger in them. I did not understand.

The journey back was smooth enough. I had time to think. It was him or me. I needed that island, as he did. Through it, through that window, I would save myself. The last Burne-Jones. I would give Nigel the report he wanted. And I would go to London. The place would be sold within a year of my report, and then someone would buy it, anonymously. And then I'd move. We - myself and my chosen gallery - would buy the place for a song, and go public the day after. I'd have the life I'd dreamed of.

And the Association and Simon would be finished. Why did I want that, too, now? But I did.

That night in the hotel I slept more soundly than I had done for a year and, for once, my dreams were sweet. I was in the chapel. And the

Queen with the mocking eyes stepped forward with the grail and pressed it to my lips, and I drank. I understood. I could have all that I wanted. I wrote two letters. One, typed, to be faxed to Nigel. Mission accomplished. The other, by hand, I posted care of *The Sea Queen*, Penzance. Then I fell ill.

Nigel rang the morning I was back.

"I've read the report, Vivien. Good work. Shame that it was delayed by your flu. Obviously we wouldn't have bought the place if we'd been able to read your recommendations earlier. As you say, setting up our own transport out there would take us beyond the writ of the charter, whatever its attractions. Still, I'm sure we can sell it, sometime."

I waited, though each day was a greater torment. Then, four months later, Nigel made his move and put the island on the market. We sold at a slight profit to a firm of solicitors, and Nigel acquired a Jaguar. That day I resigned from the trust.

This time the skipper greeted me, offering the same salute I had seen once before.

It was an easier crossing. The whisky was gone from the window but Simon had left it in the cupboard for me. A farewell present. Now I have the solitude I have craved for so long. One day I will leave, to what, I don't know. The Association will look after me. For now, I have time.

And I am starting to heal.

On Writing

I'm really sad, feeling it slosh around inside me, a surge or pull or tide, a sickness or pain, an overburden, a ship listing with water inside it, dragged down on one side into introspection, self hatred and despair, and on the other side, hauled up…

So I'll write a poem. I reach then for the pen in the same way that I used to when I was adolescent, but what comes out doesn't go very far – one is only using words as a funnel, a harness to give direction to a stream of muddy energy. All is self-descriptive.

The movement is completely different from that which began, I suppose, with 'St David's': the feeling of place and of Strix and that I can sense a poem in there, in that tension and juxtaposition of ideas, the twist of emotion, that I stumble across, but is outside me.

Even if it is my own experience, it is outside me. I come across it as an aesthete. I'm looking for it in the jewel in the mud, the tight cluster of words which offers prismatic tension and harmony.

Poems come from here, generated by images, by thoughts making a sense of their own – dancing – beginning to oscillate or give out a musical note.

What can I say of, or learn from, the other thing – the lurch to the drunken pen?

from
Ice Maidens (2006)

Aubade

Tonight I am driving you back
to be with your real dad for the New Year.
Parker at your service, Lady Penelope.
You roll your eyes. *Whatever.*
You lie on the back seat, long legs bent
under swathes of duvet, your face
candy striped in the orange play of streetlamps,
the skin inside your wrist so white that, when
we stop, it takes the faintest sheen
of red, then green.
If I could drive you anywhere,
where would it be? *Florida.*
In Britain? *Whatever . . . You choose*

I watch you in the mirror, stretching
the seat-belt's tense embrace, tangling
headphones in your hair. Your eyes are closed
before I reach the empty motorway, slip
into that alien country that is the last night
of the year. Tonight there are no police,
no trucks, no roadworks, only
a scattering of fugitive cars, cats' eyes
streaming like tracer and once the splash
of rockets in amethyst and gold.

You're restless in your sleep, your feet
kicking my back as 'Sailing By' begins.
M5 THE SOUTHWEST. There's time
tonight for three hundred miles
before the dawn; enough to reach

Cornwall and the Lizard, Goonhilly,
its barbed wire glittering with ice,
the scarlet pulse of warning beacons;
time, as night thins to grey, to reach
the silent square where fog condenses
on rusting postcard racks and ice cream signs;
Cornish Gems, its window hushed

with velvet boxes promising
serpentine and iron pyrites; time

to reach the cove before the sun
flares pink through winter mist, to stop
and wind the window to the lash of spray,
the numb kiss of salt, to watch,
as the car grows cold, the waves,
your eyes' first flicker.

Reading Your Lips

Your timing perfect, you have slipped
to the ladies, leaving me poised
between coffee and dessert, fantasy
and fulfilment. So I hold the long handled
spoon you held, an inch from your lipstick,
as you spoke, paused, almost embraced
the heaped mound of cream, ice cream,
hot chocolate fudge, then waited,
and spoke again, hesitated, opened to take it -
and again delayed, tormenting me until
I took it from you, guided it between
your opened lips, felt it press the soft
flesh within, your tongue teasing
and releasing a mouthful of pleasure,
then as I withdrew, the soft, slight
tug as your lips pouted to suck
it clean. I do not know if, after this,
we will go home together.
It no longer matters.

Devon Churches

You keep looking for it, a place so still
that, after the door's echo, you can hear
a lark, a tractor fields away, aisles filled
with the cold quiet shock of others' prayer:
that pause. The saints in the late August
sun bleeding scarlet stains across the face
of an unplastered wall, the soft white hush
of dying lilies. As though some other place
were near, held between breaths, as, in the glass
Adam is held in the red clench of scales;
as though in the damp book you'd find, at last
a cryptic hint of some elusive grail,
the confirmation of this search: some guide,
some word or name, a sign you recognise.

Waterhouse

Beneath the water's face he finds
in these green depths the soul refracts
like light, sees in his rippling eyes
the world within, self upon bright self
breaking to his sight.So the artist
turns from love to the lure of water
and illusion, the gaze of painted
creatures meeting his own gaze.

The women he desires he bathes
in this same stream, flowing
from canvas to canvas, making
of them mermaids, sirens. They gleam
between tall reeds, milk-white naiads
playing among the waterlilies,
dragonflies. Imploring pools lap
at their childs' breasts. Just once,

as Hylas, he came to the brink
of caressing these pink-nippled
girls, the nymphs he thirsted for.
Yet as their hands, cold as river
pearls, reached to draw him
down, he knew some colours
move only in water, are seen
only by those who drown.

At Vindolanda

floods spill through tarpaulin shrouds, burst
over lawns and paths. Oaks bend
before storm water's weight. Three girls run across the ruins,
feet sodden, their faces masked and glinting
in clear plastic macs, pearl eyed
with rain. Exhumed from these earthworks
the first letter between women, its cursive script
stripped from centuries of mud's discretion: *I offer*
prayers for you, Lavinia, at the temple of the nymphs.

All along the wall, each mile fort has its shrine,
each villa a sacred well: the legions surrendering
to the cold communion of the springs, drinking
in the lapping voices of outlandish spirits,
till every river's name invokes a Goddess.

The girls twirl in a swirling hail, hold up
cupped hands, squeeze under ropes, splash
in the open dig. Their plebeian feet
churn the quarters of centurions and priests.
The sky falls, whirling down to three wide open
mouths. Prised from fresh dredged graves,
the statues are paraded under hot museum lights:
Local Deities, Water Spirits, Nymphs of the Springs.
Between this water and the sculpted stones,
some living thing that we have lost. But here,
in Vindolanda among the nymphs,
I remember how on the frontier

of sleep you came to me, night by night, holding me
breathless, appearing then as you were, once,
in the azure glare of underwater lights: the crossed straps
scarring your pale shoulders; the wet veil of hair
slashed across one cheek; tight drops
scaling your tensed thighs, reptilian,
beautiful; the cup of shadow offered
at the hollow of your collar bone; you,
balanced, as herons balance on the brink

of killing. Or some discarnate thing,
which, as you dived, you yielded to,
till your blue nails tore the water's skin,
splayed across the tiles; and after them your face
rising, broken and baptised
in the mosaic flickering of light.

My clothes are a shell of water.
There is no one here, no-one but the three girls,
splashing, unafraid; above, the pregnant clouds,
piling and coiling, murmuring in the soft breath
of gods that is like the sound of boulders
falling. The tarpaulins stretch
to bulging pouches, growing.

Strix

Home again, and sleepless, a cry outside
comes like a memory. As children
we would wake in the illicit hours, lie rapt
in the night that vibrated on two cold notes:
owl call and silence. Older, we ventured
to the trees, strained our throats to answer,
our rough owl words half way to witchcraft.
So all have conjured syllables of your tongue
to cast your name. Saxons called you *ule*,
Normans, *hulet*; monks, hearing your scream
scored through their vigils, transcribed
the consonants like claws: *strix*.

Nana

A farm, pitched like a ship
against the hail of seaspray on cliffs
eaten year by year by the malicious tide.
Upstairs, one bedroom wall is window,
a slow hour glass filling with the sea.
And at this rising, sinking line
Nana, a hundred years dead
and nine years old, kneels to stare,
measuring endlessly time she cannot feel.

All who have come here, gazed
on this bleak shore have sensed it,
that line of ending, ebbing and drawing near.
Here, men dug with their own hands,
the bones of deer, raised stone slabs
above their dead, slanted to the setting sun.
The Celts called these bruised, weed-stained
reefs Caer Arianrhod, poised between life and life,
death and death. Here the knell of Christ
tolled to mark the road to the isle of pilgrims,
where the brown limbs of saints are laid,
thick as apple roots beneath the spade.

So at my own death, I may recall
these fields with their rusting fence,
this tattered swell that weeps and fills, these deeps
where time is held in store among the waves.
Once more then, perhaps, I'll see her, her image
flat against the patient light: Nana,
still watching, waiting, for that final bell
to wake her into freedom, into sleep.

Nimue

And when he left her she climbed the cliffs
of serpentine and granite, found
the secret place where adders sun themselves,
cross hatched with menace and allure, snake
upon snake basking in glistening coils.
She lay among them in the hot breath
of thyme and samphire, slept. As she dreamed,
she heard the swift burst of the surf, felt the heat
of rock beneath her, the sun's heat
on her back and still another flame
as though not just the sun had scorched her,
but, added to its strength, the red fires
of Aldebaran and Antares, Draco and Serpens,
rising from the dark of summer stars.
When she woke she watched the waves
writhe their rippled backs into the strand.
In the evening she rose to face a scarlet sun,
holding his heat within her; waited, silent,
at the chapel in the cove among the wives
of fishermen; ate the thin wafer
from the priest's cold hand.

Morgana

We will inherit that land of poppies, pomegranates
the bright isle which drowning men have seen
as the last darkness parts before their sight,
which rests, they say, beyond the furthest west,
but lies, in truth, beyond the stark horizon
at every compass point; to which the soul must turn,
quivering to stillness.

And while from that glittering sea we turn our eyes
it sends its signs to us: the hush
after birdsong in the dusk, the red sun
sinking beneath the earth, and at the mass,
looking from face to face, we see its light there,
as each sips the blood of the eternal kingdom.

Apples, and apple wine, brewed sharp and sweet
as the serpent`s kiss, scents of cinammon and clove
twine round the trees of those green glades
where we will meet again with those we loved,
and know them beautiful, as in their youth,
or in the hour when they were most themselves.

Igor

shrugs, lifts a single finger, contemptuous.
Eskimos? In Russian there is one word
for snow, schoolteacher. This -
He jerks a thumb at the fields of drift ice,
its grey redeemed only by the distant yellow
excrement of walrus, the red-brown excrement
of seals, at pyramids, arches, thrown up
by chance collisions of floe on floe. On the port bow,
an aquamarine cathedral, glistening,
tortured into spires. *It is ice, yes ?*
Why do you want more words?

On Igor's watch, while the crew sleeps
in endless light, between SatNav, radar,
radio, the log, he teaches me fragments
of latitude, depth charts, the sea.

Half my age, he commands
ice strengthened vessel *Akademic Kaplinsky,*
registered Murmansk, bends course to chase
whales for me, tells me
of the Naval Academy Planetarium:

They take you in there - it is dark.
They show you one constellation -
just one. They say, what is that star ?
We have to learn one hundred stars.

Ny Alesund

This is the end of the world.
Here, the last shop, the last
telephone. In Pyramiden,
Longyearbyen, they said,
North of here there is nothing,
nothing but Ny Alesund, and its scientists.

And at Ny Alesund there is, indeed, nothing
but North itself.

In the winter, bears come from the hills
grey in our arclights, overturn
the skips, eat our sweet
garbage. We hear the frenzy
in the dog-pens, watch
from first storey windows.

Afterwards, in their excrement we find
aluminium foil, shreds of tin cans;
once, the year the tourists
died, the zip of a cagoul
of German manufacture.

In Ny Alesund, we celebrate
our latitude, display it
on mugs, sweatshirts,
78° 56' North.
Two hundred metres from the pier,
the post office. Four hundred metres
from the pier, wilderness.
You are forbidden to leave Ny Alesund
unless you bear a firearm,
minimum 7.62 calibre.

The government posted an inspector here.
Each night he drank, then he stole
a car, drove round and round the village.
A helicopter had to come for him
from Barentsburg: pilots, aviation fuel,

two thousand dollars. They made him pay for it,
then charged him with theft, misuse
of government property, and professional
misconduct. Technically he had committed
no traffic offence as there are no roads here
that meet international definitions.

From Ny Alesund, there are only two
directions: the pole, and failure.
We come after those who follow
the explorers, coming as far
as they can after their sons,
fathers. Frost welds their crucifixes
to the list of etched and absent names.
The marble busts of Amundsen
and Nobile stand at the edge of town, look out
on nothing. A plaque:
A Tutti Gli Esploratori Polari
di Ogni Tempo e Ogni Nazione.

In the winter, the helicopter comes
once a fortnight, bringing newspapers
from Tromso, scientists, marmalade.
When the weather is bad it does
not come, and in the winter the weather
is usually bad. It is advisable to bring your own
supplies of anything you may need.

Our two hours has expired; we must go
North. The harbour master
talks to the crew in Russian, flirts
in Norwegian with the officers,
waves us off. Above her office
she has written a sign.

Ny Alesund. 78° 56' North.

Polar Hotel

Welcome to the United Nations Conference
on the Preservation of Arctic Mammals!
Main course whale steak in garlic sauce.

Ocean currents are concentrating pollutants
in arctic waters to toxic strength.
Tonight, Bar Special: Arctic Cocktails!
White rum and vodka with glacier ice.

Many of you have travelled here to see a Polar bear.
Svalbard has the highest quantity
of bears in Europe. If a bear arrives,
you must leave immediately.

Guests are advised not to exit the hotel
without a firearm which can be hired locally.
It is prohibited to carry loaded weapons within
dining room, bedrooms or sauna area.

Carry this guide with you at all times.
Bears may be hungry or curious.
A curious bear will be a threat
only if it regards you as a food source.
Do not run from a curious bear.

If a bear comes near you, shout
and wave your arms. This may scare
a curious bear, but is ineffective
against a hungry bear. In the spring
all bears are hungry. Do not run. Shoot flares.

Do not shoot flares behind the bear
as this may prompt an attack.

If a bear comes within a hundred metres
take off items of clothing and throw them.
This may delay a curious bear.

If the bear comes within fifty metres, do not run.
The bear is a protected species.
Shoot it repeatedly in the chest area.

Below fifty metres chance of survival
is low The bear can travel at speeds
of up to 50km / hr so running
will not be effective.

Avoid all intimate contact
with wild animals.The island
is a rabies infested area.

Wildlife is protected by international treaty.
Shooting of bears is a criminal matter
and will be investigated by the authorities.
Failure to report may lead to imprisonment.
Note the sex of bear and if possible its weight.

In the event of death of persons
this must be reported to the Governor
during working hours.

Oviedo

Fiesta. In the hotel, one attic room
was left. Among madonnas, candles,
lamps, a handle in a wall of glass
opened to my key, and, through the looking glass,
a loft where a century's self-doubt
lined slanted walls. As though it were a sin
to cast away a mirror or a saint:
they had this place. Their angled gaze
crossed and double-crossed, framing
each other into infinity, stretching
further than my eyes dared. Then you came there.

As we touched, I watched my hands caress
the hair of one whose face was hidden,
betraying you with her, but we moved together
to see our twins in those other silvered rooms
break their incestuous embrace to gaze at us
wide-eyed. Their startled smiles made us
smile, till they, as we, turned to kiss.

That night I woke on a double bed, in the cold calm
of mirrors, found us back to back, like children
joined at the spine, your foot's sole pressed
to mine, the heart's symmetry written in our flesh.

Good Friday

She enters. Her heels rap the marble floor.
Her coat sweeps her ankles.
Above, a flood of leaded darkness
presses the outlines of the saints.

Charcoal flickers scarlet on the altar
We gather at the rail.
The priest pushes five brass daggers
into the candle's yielding wax.

We sing. We breathe in incense, dizzy.
We summon into the candlelight
the lamb crucified, a severed ear, a kiss.
Somewhere a wound is pierced.

We kneel. She takes the silver chalice
in gloved palms, inclines her head,
drinks, wipes the rim clean
of lipstick, holy blood. We rise,

embrace, her fingers sheathed
in leather, her upturned collar
brushing my cheek, her breath
a psalm of scent and wine.

Speaking in Tongues

Are you sure, Fiona asks, you're not a priest? Ten minutes left
before her next, and she lies on her back, knees bent up, her red hair
fanned across the lilac sheet, dabbing her chest with a wet wipe.
I pour her a warm coke. Outside it's eighty-eight degrees; inside,
the fan grinds back and forth. From one wall come the usual sounds,

from the other, Caprice, ten hours into a twelve hour shift, saying,
trust me, it happens all the time. Have it your way, Fiona says,
I've been around too long. They come in here around Lent,
the young ones, before they take their vows. And then I see them after.

Two pigeons flurry at the skylight, fall exhausted and Caprice
is trying again when Fiona says, You know this place was haunted?
Lights coming on and off, ashtrays flying round. All that stuff. Bloody
punter, of course. Dead and nowhere better to hang around than here
the bastard. Didn't bother me. I says, *if you can move plates about,*
why don't you do the bloody washing up? But the wee girlies
were getting frightened. Voices. Touching their hair. And then it's bad

for business. So there's this one guy - one of my regulars. I had a feeling
about him. I didn't ask, cause then it makes it awkward. I just says
to him, *I've got this problem. Now could you maybe do something,*
just as a favour ? Looks that damn surprised, I tell you.
Then all serious, he says *I'll need to be alone, Fiona.*
She passes me some tissue, sips her coke, and I see

him standing in this room, naked, his right hand lifted, quartering
the air. His breath slowing, the pulse of the fan, the cars outside, all
slowing, beginning the Liturgy of Deliverance and as he speaks
something growing present, clawing at his nerves, a burden in the air
an outline at the edge of vision, the muscles in his neck
tensing, sweat glistening on his temples, running in the hollow
of his spine and then, unasked, his throat convulsing, saliva

flooding in his mouth and breaking in the room the tongue
of angels, harsh with the arid rhythms of the desert
the air opening to his words the way that eggshell opens for a bird
or snake. His palms scorching and all this, the bed,
the table with its folded towels, the plate of Durex, Asda talc, blazing
holy, their colours scalding, the light of every thing awoken, and then the peace

of nothing, the carpet, walls, fading to dullness, and him standing here, the air chilling on his skin, the damp prints of his feet, his hair matted, limp, and outside the shrill summons
of the pelican lights on Dundas street.

Right enough, Fiona says, he did the job. Not that I'm religious - Christmas and weddings, me. But I could tell, he'd cleared it out. *I owe you*, I says to him and then he says to me *Fiona, you realise,* he says, *I'm really sorry, hen. I can't come back here now.*

Lorrayne

Her life is full of miracles. *Things happen,*
and it's, like, I've dreamed them before ?
Last week she found a DVD player
among the binbags on her street. *It works.*
Honest? Her horoscope warns when to go out,
black cats which streets not to walk.
It's intuition? There's some cars
you just don't get into, you know ?

I've pulled in out of sight, among the rubbish,
squares of shattered glass, the site
of some old factory, a house.
Will you do my cards for me, after?
The wipers flog the dark, then die,
folded on each other. She's painted now
by every fleeting light, her arms thin mirrors
to the orange radiance of halogen. The beams
of distant cars sweep her pale back.
Could you make it thirty-five?
I've got to pay the rent. The handbrake
warning light – a single angry
exclamation mark - bleeds onto her palm.
Her hair is wet as rags.
My boobs are better now – see?
Tattooed on one small breast, a tiny heart
in red. *I smell alright, don't I?*
Between her thighs her flesh
starves into hollow curves. As she moves
my hands clasp three tight ribs
in each cold span.
It's only girl smell, isn't it?

Afterwards I lay for her, crowded
on the seat, the Queen of Rods, the High Priestess.
Don't worry, I won't touch them.
They're good cards, aren't they?
As I drive back she takes my sweets,
tells me of the shoes she's seen for twenty pounds
in TJ Hughes; the guy who paid her

to smear her feet with spit and walk on him;
her friend Sam, raped by two men in an Audi.
Her mum. Her eyes meet mine, dead level
as she talks. When she gets out she says,
You take care now. There's bad girls
out here, all kinds.

Homecoming

Another hour of driving, sleeping farmsteads,
jagged turns, and then this garage, its lights
an island in the dark. I pull over, step out, lost,
unsteady in the forecourt's glare, the darkness
of the mountains crowding round, the pumps beaded with rain.
The whirr and throb of diesel, the wind
filling the silence.

There's been no sign. But in the kiosk, Tunnock's Teacakes,
Mackie's milk, the Herald: *Fifth Vice Girl Murdered;*
the border elided somewhere in the night.
My way from here is mapped:
TOWN CENTRE, TOURIST ROUTE:
persistent street lamps fading in the dawn;
the moment when the sun first strokes the trees;
my road; huge skies, clouds piled in slate
and white and blue; deerfences and Dutch barns;
crows flapping from the verge; pylons ranged
for miles across the fields;
the sweet heaviness of barley in the dew.

Coed y Farden

I

Coed y Farden: three square miles where no one comes
by foot, or land-rover, for days on end :
bounded by crumbling dykes and rusting wire,
the river choked with flashflood branches;
lines of pines and spruce broken, thinned
by fifty years of storm, their fallen trunks
opening ragged glades to ash and rowan
seedlings of oak and holly: no longer
forestry plantation, not yet wild wood.

A place where silence holds
within it the surf-surge of the spruce, the mutter of water,

yet rests unbroken, its stillness
not absence of sound
but strands of quiet through which the place itself listens:

the soft pad
as drifts of needles yield under my boots;

the changing in the river's voice
as I cross its current, the way it closes back again;

the flat chime of barbed wire springing back
vibrating from post to post into the soil.

II

It's only here I know
this cleanness of the air, of pine and peat

Here under the rain, a cold stone at my back,
there whispers at the edge of thought a sense

of subtle territories of blood and scent
a cigarette smoked half a mile away,
the taint of diesel and exhaust
lingering on the track for hours
after the foresters have gone
a stillness that has me turning, sometimes
to the crow's flight before I hear it

sometimes to see nothing
visible.

Lives which compass mine
the way the buzzard's circles hold
the lesser worlds of rook and heron;

which intersect with mine only the way
the mud at dawn unites the tracks
of fox and polecat, their hunger hours apart.

III

It's only here that I acknowledge
that this is my religion,
underpinning everything, this bond
I've made with you and never spoken,
that you understand runs deeper
than any marriage, a kind of parenthood,

in which your spirit finds no rest
but still a place to venture from
and to return. A faith
whose confirmations are all ambiguous:
voices in the wind;
an empty bed: mud on the stairs;
the grit your tongue discovers
between your teeth.

It's here, in Coed y Farden, that I believe
this love, patient, unforseen, may redeem
all that is merely human, its proof
absolute discretion; the tenderness
of ordinary things: to wait
in the tired dawn and watch

for your eyes opening; to dress
the scratches on your limbs;

return you to your name.

January

Leaving the house before dawn, returning
late, my home becomes for weeks on end

a place of darkness: cold owl call greeting me
after the slam of the car door; the moment's

exhalation and relief. Then with the in-breath
frost burning in my throat; my neighbour's

woodsmoke; the silence of Sirius singing
in the branches of the ash, the world

large again. All this month I have come
to bed knowing I have achieved

nothing, nothing to save from the day
that has passed but ragged minutes

of prayer, thanks spoken and pleas
offered beneath Orion and Auriga

to spirits I cannot name. They come,
or seem to come, answering

to fire and air, teach me to find
their eyes in the blurred glimmer

of the stream I know now
only by moonlight or darkness. I hear

their voices in the swirl and clink
of the river as it thickens with ice.

Each night I have stood in mist or rain
at the same bend in the road, the same patch

of trodden mud beside the gate,
till persistence or exhaustion has worn

thin whatever ether lies between
my clumsy desires and their searing

tenderness. Until, it seems, it is they
who come between fields and stars,

summoning, and I who answer.

Extracts from the Journal

Still I give thanks for the extraordinary gifts that have been mine, and first on the list have been Christina and the girls. Those moments of thankfulness, so many of them, by the river, by particular trees, and other more wild, random ones, just pausing, stopping in Liverpool, or driving, thinking – hey, this is amazing, I've got so much. Those moments light up for me now, a chain of coloured lanterns, tiffany green, of bright jewels where the substance of happiness did not just rush by but was caught, at least in my own mind, like crystals whose hearts were flaming water – an emerald chain of light, not just absorbed or illuminated but held up, reflected.

The Bible is always talking about thanks, but oddly now I'm starting to think that I have always misunderstood what was going on – that it was like paying the rent - this endless insistence on settling dues - all about obligation, doing, you must do your duty. Get down on your knees, say thank you. Because you have to.

But in fact there is some magical, divine element in thanksgiving, some secret gift tied up with it – some avenue for the soul.

It is meant as a gift for us, not as a reward to heaven. There is something within an act of praise – which is perhaps just a moment when you still yourself and hold within it. Perhaps to give pause or give thanks is in a way to make a poem – to seek out the crystal latticed way in the heart of the moment.

When you open yourself to a moment of the heart in such a way that it springs into words, you maybe touch it at a deeper level. You both know it and know its specialness at the same time.

Or, as Tolkien would say, you are a subcreator.

Maybe that is what is special, mystical, in the sense of the seventeenth century mystics – their green thought in a green shade, their bright sense of God as hard, sharp in his immediacy. It cannot be that only poets do this. It is perhaps that poetry fixes, as in a photographic fixing chemical, making certain yet still.

Poetry is the outward sign of something else here. I cannot get much beyond this, not beyond these three thoughts – that it is something to do with being both inside and outside a moment, living it and knowing it at the same instant; that it is something to do with time – or with capturing the eternal; and that these moments of awe are themselves redemptive, infinitely precious. God, or the Goddess, offers us thanks as a secret bright doorway through the wall into the very treasure house of her wealth.

Perhaps these moments are pointers to what all of life could be – theoretically, for those not fretted by care and worry and bills and the daily business of fear and anxiety.

So one thought I have is about how you can take with you whatever you do take with you – which is to say, any moment which burns with the light of the eternal does become yours for eternity.

Loyalty

Amongst all virtues, loyalty is the one I prize highest.

Loyalty is the acceptance and enactment of an invisible bond.

Loyalty demands loyalty. Not in a demanding way, but in the way that the sun demands that the autumn day is warm : it makes it so.

Loyalty is a celebration of something sacred – that beyond the calls either of duty or of self interest, there are sacred gifts – the gifts of friendship and of gratitude.

Loyalty is a strong rope to hold onto in the darkness.

Loyalty is the knowledge that somewhere over the hill there is a safe place, a fire lit and a meal served, though you cannot yet see it.

Friendship

The two things that are the greatest are love, and the loyalty that springs from love.

It was said by one of the Christian philosophers I think – or Aristotle – that there are three kinds of friendship. There is friendship founded on mutual self interest. There is friendship founded on enjoyment of the other's company. And there is friendship founded on a common knowledge of the good. Let us say then, on a common understanding of what is good.

I think there are friendships of convenience, and those of spirit. Friendships of spirit are the most precious gift and they are rare.

A friendship of convenience has this in common, everywhere – that meeting outside your common circumstance, you have almost nothing to hold you together. A friendship of spirit has this in common – that you can pick up with someone a year, ten years, after you last spoke to them or met them, and that the bond that you have will still sparkle, because it is a true thing between you.

Give your friendships room to grow. If you settle into the lifetime that is a friendship, then that lifetime will have far times and near times. There is time to lose friends for a while, knowing that the tug that is within you both will draw you back. Be always forgiving of what may cross or distract a friendship.

The sacraments of friendship are company, and place, and gifts. Don't be afraid to buy presents out of all order, out of all rhyme and season, if you see something to make such a friend happy.

Wilderness

Moment of insight last night. A bit weak, drifting, there came to me the hawks who come over the chapel in the summer, drawn from the Berwyn glyns to circle over the fields, crying to each other. The lazy tranquillity of those warm evenings, the sense of being slightly included in the wilderness, because we, the river and the fields are now under the reign of the hawks.

And following from that, a sense of the importance of this place where we live, of there being a reason for us being in the heart of the place we are in. Not a clear reason, but a purpose half-hidden, tangled up, concealed. And in part deliberately held back by the land. The dour farmers, the language that we are still outside of, the thorn hedges and fences, gates laced with extra barbed wire. It has not been a welcoming land. But against this, last night, came the sense that those moments of opening, of welcome, were through slow persistence of our being there.

I have felt great peace – watching the clouds drift over the hills, and up by my rock, and by the waterfall, and by the moonlight in the summer, it has seemed like a true gift to be here. I still feel essentially lifted up in spirit when I pull up at the head of the glen, get out and breath in. It is mountain country, as surely as the Cairngorms is – the wild otherness of the spirit there, the absolute sense that this is no longer human territory, but the territory of the wilderness, that the animals, the trees, are the natural inhabitants and that we do not primarily belong there.

And the other thought, that hidden in these hills – 'our souls' sight too gross to glimpse it' – is a magic, and that I've been on the edge of that magic, not having understood it, but last night being aware of it. That Imogen and Amber will live naturally within it and that it will enfold them, teach them its secrets. I became part of the lanscape of Bieldside, knowing it as my only and natural world, and discovering it as I discovered myself. My parents, from their own worlds, never had that. But for the girls, this is their world. And the things I've understood about the magic specific to North Wales – my Blodeuwedd work, my Bodeuwedd dream – have taken me near enough to know the mystery is there. And last night my poem about Pryderi at the Caer, the promise that there IS a citadel of magic, a spiritual realm, tangled and mazed in these hills. That is the meaning of that Branch of *The Mabinogion* and it's a meaning which has touched my imagination.

A tribute by John Burnside

Shape shifters

i.m. Edmund Cusick

It was more of an art than we thought:
not how we slipped from one form to the next,

but how we forgot, in an instant,
the shape we discarded,

the old self bundled away
to the kingdom of others.

Another sense of what we mean by grace
this leaving ourselves behind, like empty shirts

filling with light and wind, at the water's edge:
dusk in the trees, and the swimmers already gone,

their eyes and voices
hurried into darkness.

Meanwhile, a hedge fills with bees, or a meadow reveals
a changing map, precise as any

magic trick
                                    while somewhere in the grass
a song emerges, or a silence blooms,

and, one by one, the bodies come to light:
this knot of gold, that skew of red and silver.

'Shape shifters' was written in memory of Edmund Cusick...a poet with whom I shared a number of interests, including the sub-Arctic, and the myths and stories of those who inhabit that region; he also had a fascination with angels, or those angelic forms whose capabilities included divine utterance and shape shifting. He once asked me if I had ever met a shape shifter, and I could see in his eyes that this was a serious question. For Edmund, I always felt, Rilke's angels were immediate and actual presences.

Edmund Cusick was a fine poet who had only just begun to overcome the diffidence that was so familiar to those who knew him.

Acknowledgements

First, I wish to express my gratitude to Christina Cusick for permission to print the work of Edmund Cusick, both previously published and hitherto unpublished writings.

Especial thanks to Dr Mark Wynn, Senior Lecturer in the Philosophy of Religion at the University of Exeter, for 'A Memoir'.

For her Introduction to the selection from *Gronw's Stone: Voices from The Mabinogion*, my thanks to the poet Ann Gray, and appreciation of her careful work in preparing some of the unpublished poems for publication.

I am grateful to Patricia McCarthy, Editor of *Agenda*, and to John Burnside, for kind permission to print his poem '*Shape shifters*', first published in *Agenda, Vol 42: Nos 3 - 4: A Reconsideration of Rainer Maria Rilke.*

For the extract included in 'On Myth', from *The Writer's Workbook* (Arnold, 2000), my thanks are due to Jenny Newman and Aileen La Tourette (co-editors with Edmund Cusick), and to the publisher.

For the extract 'On Poetry' from the Introduction to *Firesigns* (2000), my thanks to the poet Rose Flint, and her publisher, Poetry Salzburg.

I also wish to record my gratitude to Georgina Gilmore, Curator of Fine Art at the Royal Pavilion and Museums, Brighton & Hove for assistance and permission to reproduce 'The Ice Maiden' by Edmund Dulac, on the front cover of this book.

I am grateful to Elaine Wilson for her careful work in typesetting part of the text and her general helpfulness.

Especial thanks to Gareth Creer, Head of Creative Writing, and to my many friends and colleagues at Liverpool John Moores University, for their support and encouragement.

'Speaking in Tongues' won the Keats-Shelley Prize 2005.
'Ny Alesund' won the Housman Prize 1998.

'Vivien' was first published in *Pool: New Fiction from Liverpool John Moores University*, edited by Maureen Duffy (Headland, 2000).

The Editor

Gladys Mary Coles is a poet, literary biographer and anthologist. The most recent of her ten collections are *Song of the Butcher Bird* (2007) and *The Echoing Green* (2001), both with Flambard. Her poetry is anthologised by Faber, HarperCollins, Virago, Seren and in the Forward Books of Best Poems. She has received the Daily Post and Liverpool Echo Arts Award for Writing and a Welsh Arts Council Writer's Award. Winner of the Aberystwyth (University of Wales) Open, the Felicia Hemans Prize (University of Liverpool) and major prizes in the National Poetry Competition, the Cardiff Festival, the Scottish International and others, she was selected to represent British poetry in the Euro-Literature project. A tutor in Creative Writing at Liverpool's universities and regularly for Ty Newydd, the National Writers' Centre for Wales, she is Managing Editor of Headland Publications.